Why Christian Speaks

Christian Proffit

Acknowledgements

First, I would like to thank God. Without Him this wouldn't be possible. Thank you for opening my eyes and allowing me to see my calling.

I would like to thank my beautiful children, Daniel, McKenzie, and Mason. You guys are my motivation and inspiration in everything I do.

I would like to thank my sister, Macarro. You believed in my vision and helped me bring it to light, and for this I am forever grateful.

To all my friends and family, especially my brothers and sisters, for believing in me. Thank you for giving me feedback and insight when needed. I extend my endless appreciation.

I would like to thank my good friend, Tasha, for keeping me on my toes when I needed that extra push.

Last but not least, I would like to thank Paul. Thank you for your endless encouragement, love and support.

Dedication

This book is dedicated to my granmommy, Hazel Laurent. I know you are smiling down on me. Your selflessness will always be remembered. Thank you for being there for me, and always loving me. I love and miss you so much.

Why Christian Speaks

-Memoir-

Introduction

I haven't talked with many people about my past. I've always been too ashamed or too embarrassed. I've shared my life with a selected few when I thought my story could help them and let them know I understood their pain. After sharing my life experiences, I'm often faced with a similar response, "But you look so normal." Looking at my life today, I'm still a work in progress. It's hard for people to believe the life I once lived. If it didn't happen to me, I probably wouldn't believe it myself.

Staring at the woman in the mirror, I'm often disgusted with flashbacks of my past, though, in that same glance, it brings me great pride to know that through all of those struggles, I'm still here. Yes, I may look normal, but it's because I've mastered the art of hiding how I feel, carrying my war wounds deep within.

My hope in writing this memoir is to show you, the reader, that even though you may be in an undesirable situation, you can still overcome your circumstances and defeat the odds, just as I did. I'm living proof that beating yourself up for things in the past only prolongs your pain and puts off your healing. This book will have served its purpose when you are able to point out opportunities to make better choices for yourself, before it's too late.

I'm taking all of my life's experiences: poverty, sexual and mental abuse, drugs, alcohol, and promiscuity, and working through the damage they caused in order to turn my life around. I still face trials and tribulations and continue to fight daily.

Making the decision to do something different was just the beginning. When you decide to take your life in a new direction of purpose, things improve, so get ready.

You'll see that you can take all the lemons that were thrown at you and still make some damn good lemonade. Mine is still bitter, but I'm working on the recipe. Everyone has a story to tell. Whatever your story is, own it. My goal in sharing my experiences is to be an inspiration for someone to *begin* the process of turning their life around. Taking the first step to begin *any* change is often the hardest part, but it's worth it.

This is why I write... This is why, Christian Speaks.

Why Christian Speaks

******

It was a Saturday night, and Sean and I decided to go out and grab something to eat. I was in the mood for barbecue ribs and TGI Fridays had the best ribs. I thought I looked particularly cute in my white polo top and dark blue jeans. My brand new, all white Reebok Classics were fresh out of the box, and my honey blonde shoulder length hair was pulled up into a loose ponytail. I loved wearing my hair honey blonde, because it matched my golden-brown eyes. Sean stood at my side, wearing one of his colorful silk button up shirts, dark blue jeans, and a black fedora hat. I guess he was going for the mature debonair look, but he looked more like a pimp. Sean was about 6 feet tall and weighed about 200 pounds. He had a caramel skin tone with medium brown bedroom eyes to match. I must admit, my man was sexy and all the ladies wanted him. But, he was mine. At fourteen, I looked damn good standing next to this man, ten years my senior.

When we arrived at the restaurant, I was already tipsy. Due to my age, I had to have my drinks beforehand because, depending on the waitress, if they decided to card me, it would be a no go. Once inside, we requested the table in the corner near the window, away from all of the hustle and bustle of the busy restaurant. When the waitress came to take our order, I let Sean order for us both. We did this because he was older and would sometimes get away with ordering alcohol for me. He ordered my favorite: a slab of barbecue ribs with a loaded baked potato. Sean ordered the same for himself.

"Oh," he said, "and two frozen piña coladas."

"Will that be all?" she asked.

"Yes," he replied, "Thank you."

We looked at each other and smiled because she didn't ask for my ID.

Dinner was good, as expected. I must have been starving, because I ate every bite, which wasn't surprising because I've always had a hearty appetite. You couldn't tell by looking at me that I could eat more than most men. Weighing only 95 pounds soaking wet, my appetite was well hidden. Two piña coladas and a full tummy later, it was time for dessert. Being the big kid that I am (literally), I'm a sucker for sweets. I decided on a slice of apple pie and Sean had chocolate cake.

When dinner was over, Sean and I walked back to the car, acting silly, still feeling the effects of the alcohol. The parking lot was located up the block from the restaurant. We didn't mind the walk because the cool breeze was refreshing.

When we got to the car, his power locks did not work (like always), so, once he was inside the car he had to open the door for me. But, before he had a chance to open the door, a car sped into the parking lot. You could hear the tires screeching, they were going so fast. Two guys jumped out of the car, walking fast in my direction, headed right for me. They came towards me so fast, I didn't have a chance to react; I was frozen. They both wore all black and ski masks covered their faces. All I could see were their eyes, their blood shot eyes. The driver pulled out his gun and put it to my head. In a matter of seconds my life flashed before my eyes: I saw my granmommy smiling, heard my brothers' and sisters' laughter, and even saw my mother and father engage in a kiss. The feelings brought on by this gun at my head left me in a calm place.

He fired a shot.

Seconds later, I fell to the ground and my head bounced off the pavement. My eyes were still open. I saw the feet of people under the car as they ran and screamed. I heard the sirens from the *ambulance in the distance. The sounds of the*

screams were piercing. I couldn't move.

"Christian, wake up, baby! Wake up!"

"I'm up!" I answered, as I woke from my dream, shaking and breathing heavily.

"You were crying in your sleep again! Were you having another one of those dreams?"

"Yes," I replied, wiping the tears from my face.

"Are you okay?" he asked, putting his arms around me.

"Yes, I'm fine. I'm sorry for waking you up again. This shit is getting crazy."

"I know," he replied. "You want to talk about it?"

"No, I'm fine. Let's go back to sleep."

"Are you sure?" he asked, worried, tired of seeing me go through this almost every night.

"Yes, I'm sure."

"I love you my precious rose," he said, kissing me on my forehead as we cuddled together, trying to find our comfortable spot in the warm bed.

"Thank you." I planted a kiss gently on his chest. "I love you too, Paul.

Chapter One

"There are wounds that never show on the body that are deeper and more hurtful than anything that bleeds."

~ Laurell K. Hamilton ~

As I laid in the bed, wide awake, waiting for the alarm to go off, a million thoughts were going through my mind, wondering if the therapist would be an old, bald, fat man. I wondered if this would be a waste of time, if I was fixable. Damn, there goes the alarm!

"Rise and shine," Paul was singing in my ear. He was always in a good mood. I loved that about him.

"I'm up," I answered, throwing the blanket over my head.

"Were you able to get back to sleep okay last night?" he asked.

"Yes, thanks to you," I answered with a smile.

"Are you nervous?" Paul pulled the blanket down from over my face.

"No," I snapped, "I'm not nervous. Why would I be nervous?"

"I'm just asking," he said, chuckling.

"Don't forget to tell him about your dreams."

"I won't."

I walked away, thinking to myself, truthfully, I am nervous. I guess that's the best way to describe the emotions I was dealing with, either nervous or embarrassed. Whichever the case, there was a funny feeling in my stomach.

****

I arrived to the hospital at my appointed time. It was nothing like I imagined. I was a sucker for the contemporary. I loved surrounding myself with things clean and bright, and this place was anything but that. The decor was from the 1980s. Everything seemed dark and dingy. "What did I get myself into?" I asked myself, aloud.

As I entered the building, the first thing that hit me was the smell of old people and

cheap perfume. I despised the smell of cheap
perfume. The clerk at the information desk told
me that the office where my appointment was
scheduled was located in the basement. How
creepy was that? 'Now Christian,' I said to
myself, 'Have an open mind and stop being so
shallow.' So, I tried.

I took the elevator down to the
basement and looked for the doctor's office.
Reading the signs located at the entrance of
each door, I saw an office for Education,
Payroll, and Mental Health. Really? How
embarrassing! They could have come up with a
more creative name than Mental Health! It was
bad enough I had to see a therapist, but, once I
walk into this office, everyone will know that I
have issues with my mental health. On top of
that, the smell of the place was nauseating.
When I made it to the front desk I was greeted

by an older woman. She seemed nice. Her hospitality made me feel a little more at ease.

"May I help you, baby?" she asked.

"Yes, I have an appointment."

"Fill out these forms please, and I'm going to need to see your insurance card and ID."

I finished filling out the forms and when I looked in my purse to find my insurance card and ID, there was no ID! Was this a sign? Was somebody trying to give me hints that I didn't need to be there? First the 1980s decor, the creepiness of being in a basement, and not to mention that smell! I always have my ID. How was it that of all days, that day it was not in my purse? I explained to the receptionist that I could not find my ID and she accepted an expired one. I think if it wasn't for her kindness, I would have left.

"Have a seat and the doctor will be with you shortly. Okay, baby?"

"Thank you."

While I sat in the waiting room my embarrassment resumed because there was a man already there who decided to stare at me. Within seconds, my embarrassment dissipated because the realization hit me that I shouldn't feel uncomfortable about this man seeing me there, when he was there as well! He obviously had mental health issues too! His stare made this obvious.

I decide to calm down and stop letting outside distractions deter me. I was there for a reason and was going to go into this with an open mind. After about fifteen minutes (yes, he was late), my therapist came to greet me. I thought this was a nice gesture for him to greet me himself instead of having me walk aimlessly down the hallway looking for his office. The therapist did not look anything like I expected. He looked to be about 35 years old and was a little nerdy, an average build, and he wore glasses.

"Hi Christian, nice to meet you," he said, as I followed him to his office.

"Nice to meet you," I said, kind of unsure about someone so young "working" on my mental health.

His office was nothing like expected, or should I say, how offices were portrayed on TV. It was very small, but cute. He had dimmed lighting, which I assumed was to make the room calm and relaxing. His office contained his desk, two chairs (regular chairs, not the kind that reclined), and a little table where he kept his coffee and tea. I guess he wasn't too fond of the smell of that place either because he had air freshener. His office smelled pleasant.

"Here are a few forms I need for you to fill out" he said, as he handed me a clip board. "Before I begin, I must tell you something; if you tell me that you are thinking about harming yourself, the elderly, children, or anyone else for that matter, by law I have to contact the authorities."

Damn! I guess I'll keep *that* to myself. "I understand," I replied.

When I handed him back the clipboard I noticed that he was just as nervous as I was. Maybe he was new. I didn't know how I felt about that. Did I need a more seasoned therapist? Would my dysfunction scare this poor guy out of his profession? 'Shut up, Christian,' I said to myself, 'Just go with the flow.'

"So, tell me about yourself?"

I hated when people asked me that!

"Umm," I said, in an awkward tone, "What would you like to know?"

"Well," he said, looking at his computer, "First, let's go over a few basic questions. It says here on your form that you were born in 1981, so that makes you 33."

"Yes, that's correct."

"Wow. You don't look 33 at all!"

"Thank you." I guess he knew flattery would break the ice, so bring it on. Who doesn't like a good compliment?

"Do you have any children?" he asked.

"Yes, I have three. Daniel is fourteen years old, McKenzie is nine, and Mason is a year old."

"Wow," he mumbled to himself. "Let me see," he said while looking at questions on his computer screen. "What is the highest grade you completed in school?"

"I have my Master's in Psychology," I answered.

"Oh, really!" he responded with a smile. "Why Psychology?"

"Well," trying to find the words to say, "Because the mind fascinates me. Why people do the things that they do and think the thoughts they have has always been fascinating to me. I wanted to understand it better. Once I started to understand, my curiosity developed into wanting to help people."

"Okay, that's great. Wanting to help people is always good. In what ways would you like to help people?"

"I would like help people understand themselves better. I want to help people better themselves. There's so many ways I would love to help, to give back."

"That's good to hear," he replied while looking at the computer screen once again.

"Where are you from?"

"I'm from New Orleans."

"I thought I detected somewhat of an accent," he replied, "I'm from Tennessee," he said with a smile because we were both from the south.

"Yes, I picked up a little accent from you as well."

At this point I was wondering when the crazy people questions would come into play. I could tell that he was too nervous to ask the infamous question, 'Why are you here?' So, I took the lead and was ready to get down to the nitty-gritty.

"How exactly does all this work?" I asked. "I mean, do we just talk or do you ask questions?"

"Well," he said, now, more serious. "There is no one specific way to do things. Every situation is different. There are three main types of therapy and we can decide which is better for you."

He went on to explain, "Psychodynamic therapy is talk therapy. This is the kind of therapy people think of when they think of psychological treatment. This is designed to help patients explore their emotions, including feelings they may not be aware of. This helps people understand how their behavior and mood are affected by unresolved issues and unconscious feelings.

Cognitive behavioral therapy focuses on how a person thinks. Thoughts shape what a person does and how a person feels and reacts. This type of therapy focuses on identifying and changing dysfunctional patterns of thought.

Interpersonal therapy emphasizes identifying issues and problems in interpersonal relationships, and learning ways to address and improve them."

"I see," I replied, slightly overwhelmed. "The thing is, I know why I am the way I am. I know that I didn't have the best life and that's why I'm here. I feel that I need everything you just mentioned. I need help deprogramming my craziness."

He let out a slight chuckle. "That's understandable. Let's just talk. Sometimes just talking can be therapeutic, and together we can talk through your concerns. We will see if we can make sense of what's going on in that head of yours."

"Okay," I replied, slightly relieved.

"So, why are you here? What are your concerns?"

"I am here because I am tired of going through life with a continuous negative frame of mind. I feel that my negativity is somewhat of a crutch that is preventing me from living life to the fullest. My negativity causes a strain on my relationships, gives me anxiety, and prevents me from trusting. I am also here because I still have flashbacks and dreams of things that happened to me as a child, which brings back that uneasy feeling from my past. The dreams are so vivid and detailed. I hate it. I need to know if there is something that can be done to help me with these issues."

"I see. How about we start from the beginning? You mentioned your life wasn't the best. Did you have both parents in the household?"

"No, I didn't. My mother and father divorced when we were very young."

"Oh, really?" He was writing on his legal pad. "Do you remember much from those times?"

"Yes, I remember like it was yesterday. The day when the judge wanted to meet with us, we all went to court. My granmommy was even with us. I didn't understand what the judge wanted with us when they called my brother Kenan and I into the courtroom. I started to panic. I thought that I was going to throw up. I didn't want to go in that big scary courtroom without my granmommy. I didn't want to let go of her hand. She whispered in my ear that everything was going to be okay. Her words gave me the courage to face the messed up situation my parents put me in.

Once inside the courtroom, we were seated at this long brown table. The courtroom was pretty much empty except for me, my brother Kenan, the judge, and about four other people doing their due diligence. I guess the judge was trying to make us comfortable because he was being extremely friendly. With the attempt of making us laugh, he slid across the table where we were sitting. He made small talk, asking us about our hobbies and what types of books we liked to read before hitting us with the big question. He asked my brother Kenan and I which one of our parents we wanted to live with. Both of our heads were down. I know now, looking back, that we were too afraid and too ashamed to say the truth. So, we said that we wanted to live with our mother. That was such a big mistake."

"Why do you feel that was a mistake?"

"My mother was a drug addict. Not the type of addict that mostly used while partying, but a stone cold crack head like the kind you see in the projects. My mother used drugs most of her life and even throughout her last four pregnancies with me and my siblings. It's not like the courts did not know of my mother's drug addiction. I'm sure they were made aware. We had to be only about seven and nine years old at the time. We were babies. How fair was that to put the fate of our lives in our own hands?"

"Yes," he replied. "That was a lot to ask of a child."

"Yes, it was," I agreed.

"Tell me about your father."

"My dad is a good man. He reminds me of Phil Huxtable from The Cosby Show," I said with a smile. "He is about 6'3 and weighs about 250 pounds. His skin is a chocolate complexion, and he has fine, curly hair. He is very charming and everyone loves him.

My dad was physically absent the majority of my life. When he came around, it was beautiful. My siblings and I used to go to his condo and hang out in the pool all day. Those were the best of times."

"I will give my dad kudos for trying to get custody of us and get us out of our situation. But once the judge made his decision, it seemed as though we saw him less and less. I used to sit on my granmommy's porch hoping he would show up one day to save us. I can also remember thinking, who was I fooling? He wasn't coming. I don't feel that he tried hard enough to be there for us. He was only human though, and made mistakes. We were pretty much thrown to the wolves and made to fend for ourselves."

"I'm sorry to hear that," the therapist said, while taking notes. "That had to be pretty tough."

"It was," I replied.

"You mentioned your siblings. Tell me about them."

"I have a beautiful family, both inside and out. The oldest is my sister Misty and she has a son named Cory. She had a son she named Christopher, but he passed away as a baby. Misty is about 5'9 and has a beautiful brown skin tone. She's an Amazon."

"Amazon?" he asked.

"Yes. She's built," I answered with a chuckle. An Amazon is a nickname, describing a tall, built woman. Misty is a big marshmallow, meaning soft, but you would never know. She had an extremely tough exterior. People who did not know her, were immediately intimidated when meeting her. Misty had a different father than the rest of us, but she still considered our father as her dad. Misty has a special place in my heart, because she went through the most. She told me how she remembered watching the news when they were introducing the new epidemic of crack cocaine to the world. It took a while for her to understand what was happening to our mother right before her eyes. She witnessed firsthand our beautiful mother transforming into a drug addict."

"Misty had her entire life turned around in a blink of an eye. That's how easy it was for this drug to take control of our mother. The difference between Misty and Adam, and the rest of my mother's children, we were born into the world of a drug addict, so we had to learn early how to survive. Whereas, we learned to adapt to the difficult surroundings of a drug-dependent parent, Misty and Adam once had a normal life.

"When the drug addicts (our mother's new friends) would come to my granmommy's house, my sister would stand outside with her gun trying to scare them away. She thought if she could keep these people away from our mother that she would stop using. Her

thoughts were wrong."

"That's understandable. Sometimes

before an addict's family understands the

severity of their addiction they go through

desperate measures to make them quit. If only

it were that simple."

"I absolutely agree," I responded. "My

mother and sister argued all the time. She

hated what my mother was doing to herself

and our granmommy. One day they were

arguing, as usual, and the monster in my

mother arose and punched Misty's teeth out.

They were never able to mend their

relationship after that. None of us had a real

relationship with our mother. When Misty was

old enough, she left my granmommy's home

and made a life for herself and my nephew.

"After Hurricane Katrina, Misty's

mentality changed. The once hard working

mom became involved with people she would have never dealt with before. She made bad decisions and because of this, her life forever changed. It's my belief that if Misty had the guidance needed as a child, she would have had the willpower to overcome her obstacles.

"Next, we have my brother, Adam. He, along with my sister, went through the transition together with my mother. He and Misty both shared the same father. Adam resembles the singer, Maxwell. He is an extremely handsome man, and has the voice of an angel. Adam was deeply affected by the way they were living. This was evident in his actions where he would do things like torture animals as a way to release his aggression. When he was a teenager, he got into trouble. He kidnapped a woman and stole her car. I was told that money was given to my mother to help pay for his defense, but that money went straight to the drug dealer. How can you give money to a drug addict and expect them to take care of their responsibilities? Adam went to prison and was sentenced to ten years. When I was about twelve, he was released from prison and came to live with us at my granmommy's house.

"What was supposed to be a joyous occasion slowly turned into hell. The day Adam was released he was told by Misty's boyfriend that we were out of control because of our lack of guidance. He was telling the truth. That night, when Adam got home, he came into the kitchen where we all were and told us to get ourselves together or he was going to beat us straight, and this, he tried to do. He beat me and all of my siblings. He even hit my mother. One day he came into the kitchen where I was and told me that I wasn't responsible enough. Before I knew it, I was flying across the kitchen, dazed from him punching me in my face. As I was getting up from the floor, my granmommy came into the kitchen. When she noticed what he'd done, she started screaming at him. She yelled, "She is the only one who helps me! Don't ever touch her!" Adam was trying to push her out of the kitchen, but she wouldn't budge. She starting screaming for him to get out of her house. If she didn't come into the kitchen at that moment, the Lord only knows what he would have done to me. The hate we had for him was so intense that my little sister and I once contemplated killing him by putting crushed medication in his coffee. Out of all of us, Adam beat my little sister, Ava, the worst. He found a letter that she wrote to a little boy she had a crush on. He beat her with an extension cord in the laundry room, like she was an animal. Her welts oozed blood and she still wears the scars today. When I saw her when it was all over, I asked her why she didn't scream for me. I honestly believe if I had heard her screaming, I would have killed him.

"As for Adam, shortly after his release he met a girl, they married and had a baby. Everything seemed to be going well for Adam, but I guess the real world was too much for him to handle. Because Adam went to prison so young, he became institutionalized. Adam went back to another grocery store and committed the same crime again. This time, the high speed chase was captured for the world to see on TV. Once caught, he was sentenced to sixty plus years in prison. I hate to admit it now, but when he was sentenced, I felt a sense of relief come over me.

"My brother Kenan is what some would consider a 'playboy.' He has the looks and charm that drive the ladies crazy. He's about

5'9 and has an 8-pack (abs) without exercising a day in his life. Kenan has light brown eyes, and fine curly hair. One of my friends compared him to the singer, Prince. Kenan has a heart of gold and you can't help but love him. When he was in high school, some of his friends got caught up in some trouble, and to prevent the rival gang of teens from jumping on him, my mother pulled him out of school. Kenan never finished high school.

"Next, we have my little sister, Ava. Although I feel that all of my mother's children are beautiful, in my eyes Ava is simply gorgeous. She has a chocolate complexion with light brown eyes. Her features are exotic. My mother used to call us vanilla and chocolate because of our skin tones. One day when Ava was about twelve years old, her beauty caught the attention of a much older man. They exchanged phone numbers and unbeknownst to everyone, they had several phone conversations.

"One day he convinced twelve-year-old Ava to call a cab to bring her to his house. My brother saw Ava get into the cab and told my mother. My mother called the cab company and found out where the cab was going. When it was discovered that my sister was going to this man's house, my mother called the police and we met them there. Unfortunately for my sister, we were too late. By the time we made it there this man had already taken my sister's virginity. He was arrested for his actions but my mother did not fight for anything further to take place. Once all the commotion of the day was over, my mother never brought it up again. No one knows what happened to him.

"This only furthered my sister's curiosity in regards to men. When Ava was fourteen years old, she became pregnant with

my nephew. Like most people do when their
back is against the wall, Ava had to learn how
to take care of herself and her son. Early on,
Ava started stealing. She had to steal diapers
and formula for my nephew because there was
no money. Actually, my mother taught her
how to steal. When my granmommy would
send my sister to the store, my mother would
be at the door waiting for her to return with
the change. She would wet the bottom of the
brown paper bag so that it would tear, and
instruct her to tell my granmommy that the
money fell out and she lost it.

"My mother didn't make us go to
school. On days when Ava was too tired to go
to school because she stayed up with the baby
all night, I had to make her go. I refused to see
her become a teen mom and a high school
dropout. My mother was supposed to babysit
my nephew while my sister went to school, but

this would only turn into my granmommy watching him. I can recall one day (when I wasn't in school myself) my mother came into my granmommy's room, put my nephew down on her bed, and ran out of the room like it was a joke. I could tell from my granmommy's reaction that my mother did this to her often.

"Luckily for Ava and Joel, my dad did come back to rescue them, along with my nephew. I didn't want to go because I thought that I was in love with my boyfriend, Sean. I told my dad that I wanted to finish my senior year of high school and then I would come to live with him in Chicago. He agreed. As for the others, my dad met Ava, Joel, and my nephew at a McDonalds in New Orleans and took them to Chicago, unbeknownst to my mother. Once they were gone, they called my mother and let

her know they were okay. She was too high to
care.

"Last, but not least, we have Joel. Joel is
the baby of the family. He has curly hair, a
light brown complexion, and brown eyes. He
has about twenty tattoos, some located on his
neck and face.

"It is my opinion that our upbringing
had the worst effect on him. Not only was he
mentally abandoned as a child by our mother
and physically abandoned by our father, when
he became a teen, he was once again
abandoned by our father. My father brought
Joel to Chicago as a child, and when he
decided to move to Las Vegas when Joel was
about seventeen, he left him again, but this
time in the care of my little sister, Ava. Joel had
to numb himself to the world, in order to
survive his childhood, and it carried on into

adulthood. Joel is an aspiring rapper who

expresses his struggle in his music."

"Tell me about your grandmother."

"My granmommy was a God send. If it

wasn't for her, I do not know where me and

my siblings would have ended up. She stood

about 5'4 and weighed maybe 130 lbs. She had

very light skin with fine, straight hair. My

granmommy was a feisty old lady and she

didn't take any crap from anyone. Every fond

memory I have is with her. In the summer

months when we were on summer vacation

from school, I would go into her room every

morning to watch soap operas with her, and

we would watch the Golden Girls at night. One

night she called Blanche a whore, and we both

just laughed, because my granmommy never

used that kind of language. I miss those days. I

can still smell the grease she used in her hair,

and how her Secret deodorant smelled every

night while getting dressed for work. I loved
those smells, and still wear those products
today, just for the scent. My granmommy took
care of all of us. She did the best she could,
making $6.00 an hour working nights as a
nursing aid. I loved her beyond words. I miss
her dearly. My granmommy and Misty taught
me everything I know. They taught me to the
best of their ability, considering our
circumstances."

"Just like you explained about your
family, if you had to give me a brief
description of yourself, what would you say?"

"Well, everyone thinks Christian has it
all together. People assume that because I don't
complain about what I've been through or how
I'm feeling, everything is okay. This couldn't be
further from the truth. How I deal with my
pain and heartache is probably the most
dangerous of all, because I keep everything to

myself. I had to be strong my entire life and I'm so afraid of being looked at as weak, that I'd rather suffer in silence than ask for help. I had to put up this wall my entire life to shield me from the hardships of the world and now I don't know how to remove it. Finally, after thirty plus years, I'm working to remove this shield that prevents me from trusting, loving, and just giving my all."

"How are you trying to remove your wall?" he asked.

"I'm trying to trust. I'm trying to learn how to just go with the flow.

Trusting is my biggest issue, because it's causing an even bigger issue, which is my need to be in constant control."

"I see," he said, once again writing on his note pad.

I wonder, what he is writing. I wonder if I said too much. I wonder if I should have eased him into my life instead of just putting everything on the table. After all, he isn't a seasoned vet, so my issues are probably too much for him to handle. He is probably going to tell me my issues are too deep and send me packing!

"I have a homework assignment for you, Christian. I'm sure you already know that we all carry a little bit from our past, both good and bad. We all have things that we do and ways we behave that started when we were very young. I want you to take time over the next week, and write down everything that comes to mind; all of the memories that you can think of, good and bad. When you come back, we will try to dissect them and get to the root of what is having you in a not-so-good place."

"I can do that," I said with a smile. "But I'm going to warn you, you're not going to read about sunshine and lilies."

"I know," he said, chuckling. "I'm prepared for whatever you bring my way."

'Oh,' I thought to myself, 'I guess he is tougher than he looks.'

"Okay, then," I replied. "I'll see you next week."

Just like he greeted me in the beginning, he also walked me out.

Chapter Two

"One of the saddest things in life,
is the things one remembers."

~ Agatha Christie ~

I mentioned to my closest friends and family that I was going to therapy. I was met with the same response every time, laughter, but when they found out I was serious, what came next was truly a surprise. They all wanted details, so that they could cure themselves vicariously through me. The thing about people, they are so worried about what society says, no one will dare seek help for their mental issues due to fear of being criticized and stereotyped. They'd rather die silently inside and drive themselves crazy from the unknown, instead of asking for help. Because I studied mental health, I knew better. I knew I needed help, so I sought after it.

"How did it go?" Paul asked as I walked through the door. "Did you tell him about your dreams?"

"It went well," I responded in a not so eager tone.

"Well, we don't have to talk about it if you don't want to," he said.

"There's nothing to talk about, really. Today was the first day. He just asked questions about my family, and yes, I told him about my dreams."

Paul wanted everything to be instant. He probably wished I'd come back cured, that a new Christian had walked through the door. Sorry, it's still me, the same old screwed-up-mental-health Christian!

"He did give me homework, though," I said, giving him a glimpse of hope that I was one step closer to being sane. "I have to write down all of my memories so that we can discuss them next week."

Paul damn near knocked my shoulder off, finding me pen and paper to get started.

"Here you go," he said, laughing, handing me my supplies.

"Boy, stop acting like I'm crazy," I responded, laughing, taking the pen and paper out of his hands.

"You're not crazy," he told me, while putting his hands around my waist, "You're just a little off," he said, kissing my cheek.

"Well, you like my off-ness and you're stuck with my off-ness," I said, turning around to kiss him on the lips.

"No, for real, start writing," he said. "You need help? You need more pens? More paper?" he joked.

"Ha! Very funny. I'll do it when I have time, once I get my thoughts together."

A few days later, I decided to start the homework assignment the therapist had given me. I was still unsure about how much I wanted to share, because of my trust issues. I wasn't sure if I was ready to open Pandora's box. I was afraid of letting anyone close, because they would know I had a weakness. I didn't even know where to start. I had so much to say, where to begin? I took a chance and just scribbled whatever came to mind.

Families should be a source of emotional support and comfort, warm and nurturing. Family members should protect and secure each other. Notice how I said, should be? All families do not fit the above description; I know mine didn't.

I never had much of a childhood. I guess I had what they would call a hard knock life. I'm sure we had plenty of good times growing up, but unfortunately, the bad drastically outweighed the good.

Growing up, we lived in several different places with my mother. I only have a partial memory about each place, but what I do remember, everywhere we lived was filthy. The memory that I have of one place was one of the kids from the

neighborhood asking me why didn't we ever clean

up. She said every time she came over it was dirty. I

told her that we did clean up, but it got dirty again.

She said, "No, it didn't. That's the same mess I saw

yesterday" I felt so stupid, but what could I say?

She was right.

Another memory of another place we lived

was when my father came to visit. He pulled me

into the kitchen to show me the ants that were

crawling on the counters. The place was so dirty it

attracted ants! He told me that I was old enough to

clean the house. He told me there was no reason for

the house to be that dirty and I should clean it. I

was probably about eight years old. Another

memory that I have in that apartment is when we

came home one night, after being gone all day, to

find that our place had been broken into. Our house

was already so filthy and in disarray, I couldn't tell

the difference between what the robbers had done

and what was already done. I went into our bedroom and told my mother, "Look what they did to our room!" She told me that our room already looked like that. It just goes to show how we lived.

The last memory I have of one of the houses we used to live in, is when we lived on Bunker Hill Road. My siblings and I were all asleep in the same bed with my mother. I woke up in the middle of the night smelling that familiar smell. My mother was laying in the bed with her back turned to us, smoking crack. I sat up so that she could see that I saw what she was doing, but she looked at me and said without a care in the world, to go back to sleep. She didn't seem concerned at all that I saw what she was doing. Other than this, my memories are basically a blur.

The only place I ever considered home was my granmommy's house. Her house was huge. It was a big white two flat that reminded me of a plantation. There were six bedrooms total, three upstairs and three downstairs. She had a balcony on the top part of her house where we used to go out and sit. My granmommy's house was the biggest and most beautiful house on the block. It was located on O'Reilly Street in the 7th ward of New Orleans, Louisiana. That house was my granmommy's pride and joy, until we tore it apart.

My mother had six children. Four of us were born with crack in our systems. We were what the people in the hood called 'crack babies,' but if you want to get technical, we had prenatal cocaine exposure. I was told by my father that she never slowed down using drugs while pregnant with us. He said that every time she had any type of pain or discomfort from carrying us, she would just do another hit to make it all better. Because of the drug use, my sister, Ava, and I were born with some sort of nervous condition that caused us to beat our heads. Every night, when it was time to go to sleep or when we were upset, we would go to our beds and beat our heads on the pillow until we went to sleep. For some reason, beating our heads had a calming effect on us. Our mother took us to the doctor to see if there was anything they could do to stop us from doing this, but they told her that we would grow out of it. Unfortunately, it was less growing out of it and more of a substitution that took place. Since we knew that we couldn't beat our heads in front of other people at sleepovers, we developed methods that were more socially acceptable. We would rock ourselves to sleep. I still rock myself to sleep.

Growing up with a drug addict for a mother was no easy feat. Everyone knew she was a drug addict. She was the neighborhood hype. Because of her addiction, we became the black sheep of the family. Our only uncle wasn't involved with us because of his strained relationship with our mother. He couldn't stand what my mother was doing to our granmommy. Whenever we saw him, all we received was a dry 'Hi.' My granmommy's family was the only other family we knew, and we were never really close. It has always been my siblings and I; no cousins, aunts, or uncles; just us.

We were teased and ridiculed all the time by our peers. When the song "Your Mama's on Crack Rock" came out, I hated it. Every time it came on, I felt like everyone was looking and laughing at me.

My mother was once heard saying that she would never stop using drugs, and how true that was. My father used to be a drug addict with my mother, but he was able to quit. In fact, he was the person who introduced her to drugs. I guess she wasn't as strong or maybe just didn't care enough to quit. My mother's disease had complete control over her. It controlled her world. It consumed every piece of her and she didn't have room left for anything else. She wasn't there for us like we needed her to be. We didn't have her to comfort us when we were sick or to explain right from wrong.

How could she? She was sick herself. As a result, we raised ourselves.

What was sad about my mother's situation was that she once had herself together. She was an extremely smart and beautiful woman. She was about 5'9 and weighed maybe 150 pounds. She had light brown eyes and honey blonde hair. She was extremely light complexioned. She could have easily passed for Hispanic or white instead of black. She had gone to college, become a nurse and also modeled. She had her whole life ahead of her. I guess life had a different plan for her.

When my mother and father divorced, we went to live with my granmommy. She lived upstairs in the top half of the house and gave the bottom half to my mother to live with all of us. We all used to live upstairs with my granmommy and she rented out the bottom half. I guess the tenant couldn't take living with a drug addict and her children, so she eventually moved out. This was good for my mother because she had more space and freedom to do her thing. I never went downstairs. I stayed with my granmommy. Although her house was beautiful, the difference between where she lived upstairs and where we lived downstairs was like day and night. Because my mother wasn't working, the bottom half where we lived had no electricity, hot water, gas etc. My mother used electric cords that she plugged in upstairs in my granmommy's part of the house to bring electricity downstairs. This is how my mother got lights and heat. All baths had to be taken upstairs because that's where the hot water was. In the winter months when it was too cold, my granmommy would make the kids sleep upstairs in the heat.

The smell of the house downstairs was stale and it always felt damp. I don't remember anyone ever cleaning. The smell from the kitchen was overbearing because the refrigerator had molded food inside. The sink, table, and counters always had dishes filled with molded food. I only went downstairs when I absolutely had to. The front door to the downstairs house did not have a lock on it because it had been kicked in, in the past. This left me paranoid on a constant basis. I had dreams all the time of someone my mother owed money to coming in and harassing my granmommy. At night I would put the double lock on my granmommy's door to prevent this from happening. It never failed, about 3:00am my mother would beat on the door because she needed something from upstairs. Whoever opened the door had to fear my mother's wrath, mostly me, because she knew I was the one who had locked the door.

Because my granmommy was supplying energy for two homes, her bills were always extremely high. I can remember seeing her crying at the dining room table with all of her bills laid out, because she didn't have the money to pay them. She begged my mother to find a job so that she could

support her children, but this would only end up in
a fight. My mother received $600 worth of food
stamps a month for us, but she would only give my
granmommy $200. The rest she would sell and use
the money to support her addiction.

One day when my dad came to visit us, he
showed off $1,000 bands that go around cash when
you receive that much from the bank. I remember
thinking to myself, as a little girl, 'you're showing
this off, yet my granmommy is crying at the table
because she can't afford to take care of your kids!'
I'm not sure if I told my granmommy about his
money or if it was just coincidence, but she gave me
her light bill to show him. She wanted him to see
how much money she was paying every month to
take care of his kids. To my surprise, he gave me the
$300 to give to her to pay it. I was so happy to give
her that money. I was probably happier than my
granmommy was to receive it! When we were
leaving out the next day to see our father again, she

gave me the gas bill to give him. When I gave it to him he said "I'm not going to pay all of her bills!" I was so disappointed in my dad. I was ashamed to tell my granmommy he couldn't (or wouldn't) pay the bill.

Memories

My mother was a beautiful woman. Even as a drug addict, she was beautiful. When she walked, she had this sexy switch that came naturally (so she said). I noticed when she got around men, that switch became a little more pronounced, so I didn't know what to believe. Even as a drug addict, she turned heads. I learned at a young age the value of being beautiful. Because of my mother's beauty, she always had drugs. Men loved her and what she could provide them in return for drugs.

My mom had many friends; the many men that she took in the kitchen on O'Reilly Street. The man that I remember in particular was a man by the name of Ray. One day I went to get a strawberry

frozen cup around the corner from my

granmommy's house, and on the way back Ray and

I made it to the door at the same time. First, let me

say, out of all of her friends, Ray was the most

decent looking person. He didn't look like a drug

addict. He looked like a professional businessman

because he always showed up in his suit. He had a

dark complexion and wore a low afro. I thought he

must have been smart because he wore glasses. He

did not fit in with my mother and her friends. We

all knew when they went into the kitchen, doing

what they did that let loose that funny smell, they

were doing something wrong. The smell was so

distinct, I will never forget it. (Even today, when I

smell something that reminds me of it, without

thinking I say "This smells like crack." Everyone

would just look at me like, how do you know?

That day when Ray and I made it to the door

at the same time, he looked at me and said, "Fuck,

you're so beautiful. I had a girlfriend once who

looked just like you. I tried to fuck the shit out of her

in the bedroom." I just looked at him, putting on the

most innocent face that I could muster, to make him

think I didn't understand what he was telling me.

Here's a grown man telling me what he tried to do

with the woman who looked like me. At the time, I

had to be ten years old. Memories like that are the

type of memories that come to mind when I think of

my childhood.

Another memory that comes to mind was

when I was about ten years old, when my mother

allowed this stranger to come live with us, named

Tina. One night when my mother returned from the

corner store she told us that she saw this teenage

girl at the pay phone crying. My mother asked her

what was wrong and the girl told her that she had

been thrown out of her house and she was waiting

for her boyfriend to call her back. My mother gave

the girl our address and told her if he didn't call

that she was welcome to come and stay with us. I guess she couldn't get in touch with him because twenty minutes later, the girl knocked on the door. As soon as my sister and I saw the girl, we were in awe. We thought she was so beautiful. We were so impressed by this girl that we both followed her wherever she went. Weeks passed and the girl was still at our house. We heard stories of her sleeping with different guys in the neighborhood and how she won the "Get it Girl" contest at the local club by lifting up her skirt. We saw her getting in and out of cars with different men all the time and this had us even more fascinated. The more grown up activities we witnessed her doing, the more impressed we became.

One day, one of her boyfriends put her up in a little neighborhood motel. She wasn't coming back anymore and decided to let us spend one last night in the motel with her. As we were walking down the street a group of guys that she knew was walking our way. One of them put their arm around her neck in a flirting fashion and starting walking with her. Next thing we know Tina is screaming because the guy robbed her. She broke away from him and grabbed my sister and me and we began to run. She told us to hurry because he had a gun. I was so scared. I could remember thinking in my ten-year-old mind, 'Why did my mother allow us to leave with this girl we didn't even know?' I thought I was going to die that night and never see my granmommy again. For months afterward, I was terrified to go outside. I was happy she was gone because I did not want those guys looking for her and possibly killing us all. Although I was happy to see her leave, the impression she left stayed around long after. I wanted the attention I saw her attract from men.

My mother introduced drugs to the dads of neighborhood kids. I guess it's safe to say that she turned them out like my father turned her out. I would hear talk from the neighborhood that women found their husbands in our house. One of the kids told one of my brothers that our mother got their dad on that stuff.

I can recall one of her friends, who was a spitting image of Arsenio Hall, hiding out at our house from his elderly mother. I'm not sure if he stole something from her to buy drugs, but I remember them both looking out the window and ducking when they saw her car pass by.

When it wasn't easy for my mother to get her drugs, things got crazy. One night when I was sleeping in my granmommy's bed while she worked, I heard screaming outside of the window. It wasn't my mother screaming, but the guy cursing as he was punching her face. When I looked out the window I saw my mother being beat by this man in front of the shed that was next to our house. It was an actual beating. I couldn't make out exactly who the guy was, but what he was doing to her I could

make out with no question. He was punching her in
her face as if she was a punching bag. When I went
around to the front window to make sure I was
seeing this, he had already left, and she was walking
towards the house (still switching). I asked her was
she okay and she screamed at me to go back to bed.
From her demeanor, I could tell that wasn't her first
time getting beat. She acted like it was normal, as
though that beating was worth getting what she
wanted. I still have dreams of this, even today.

Another incident of my mother getting beat,
I heard from the neighborhood; how embarrassing.
Apparently when she didn't have all of the money
to buy her drugs, she took the rock (crack rock) and
bit it in half, and tried to give the drug dealer only
half the money. Word has it that when she did this,
he punched her in her face. Even though I'm sure
this happened all the time, this time was worse,
because it became the neighborhood gossip.

A memory that I have that brings about recurring dreams was when my mother took us along with her to the projects to buy her drugs. Before she got out of the car, she would tell us to lay low. We were only children, so we thought it was a game. We would lift our heads up and peek and then duck back down while laughing. Later, we would see her running back to the car, jumping in and pulling off as if her life depended on it. It wasn't until later that I figured out what she was doing. My mother was taking the drugs from the dealers and then running off before paying them. This all unfolded one day when she returned home with her face bruised and the window busted because a dealer had thrown a brick through her car window. I thought to myself, what if we'd been with her? She put our lives in danger all the time. I think she was spared so many times before because they could see us in the car.

This reminds me of the time we went to jail with my mother. One night, my mother was on one of her trips and decided to pay my dad's girlfriend (later to be wife) a visit. She piled all of her kids in the car and took us with her. When we got to the house, my mother made us wait in the car. She went to the house, beating on the door and screaming, until the lady let her in. Next thing I knew, we were all inside the house. They didn't do any screaming and fighting in front of us, but something had to be said to scare her, because she went to the upstairs part of the house and climbed out of the window. The police were called and we were all taken to jail. I was so scared. They put kids in a jail cell. I could imagine what those policemen thought of our mother as they watched over us in the cell. They felt sorry for us and gave us a pack of chocolate chip cookies for dinner. We were all so hungry, we immediately attacked our meal. Not knowing how long we were going to be there, I took the cookies and divided them amongst us, saving half the pack.

In my little mind (I was about seven or eight years

old), I thought we were going to be there forever.

Hours later, our granmommy came to our rescue.

She picked us up and brought us home with her.

Later on, our mother was released.

When my mother couldn't get her drugs,

she turned into a monster. Once she was begging

my granmommy for money. My granmommy was

telling her that she didn't have it. Not caring that

she didn't have any money to give, my mother

grabbed her purse. At this point they were fighting

over it in a tug of war. When I heard the

commotion, I ran to my granmommy's room in

time to see my mother hitting her in the head. My

mother ran away with the purse and I ran after her.

By the time I caught her she had already gone

through the purse and taken what she wanted.

When she saw me she started screaming, while

throwing the purse at me, "TAKE IT, YOU LIL'

*BITCH! YOU'RE ALWAYS TAKING HER
SIDE!" I just looked at her and said "I hate you." I
went back to my granmommy and helped her off the
floor.*

*One of the reasons I think that I have trouble
sleeping is because of my mother. She used to wake
us up out of our sleep on a consistent basis to look
out of the window and into the trees. She was
hallucinating from the drugs. She wanted us to see
the men in the trees. She told us that my father sent
men to watch us and they were doing it from the
trees. One night I got mad at Ava because she said
"I see them, Mommy!" She wanted to make my
mother happy. Once the trees weren't enough. She
started seeing people in our vents and would burst
in our room and accuse us of talking to the people in
the walls. We'd become so accustomed to this, that
just from the look on her face, we knew what was
coming next.*

The way we were disciplined was terrible. We were beat with this 2x4 piece of wood she kept in her room. If we weren't beat with the wood, she would use brooms or just hit us with her fists. In my case, this would happen when I wouldn't give her money. She would tell me that I was out fucking and sucking dick so she knew I had money. One day after I told her I didn't have any money, she snatched my gold hoop earrings out of my ears to sell. I saw her sit them on the dresser while she got dressed and I took them back. When she noticed the earrings gone, she turned psycho on me. She grabbed her 2x4 piece of wood and came after me like a mad woman. I've seen my mother violent before, but this time was like none other. After seeing the desperation in her eyes, the anger I had went away. All I felt was pity. I gave her the earrings and walked away.

One day my mother and granmommy were arguing in the kitchen. My granmommy was, once again, asking her to get a job. I guess she said

something my mother did not like because my

mother took the pot of hot coffee and threw it in my

granmommy's face. I will never forget the sound of

her voice as she screamed.

     That scream still haunts me in my sleep. I

have dreams of that day, all the time, but in my

dream, the outcome was different. In my dream, the

coffee is like acid that instantly eats away at my

granmommy's flesh. I tried to help her by patting

her with a towel, but with each pat, more and more

skin disappeared. Not knowing what to do anymore.

I just held her. I held her while she screamed and

cried.

     That is enough. These thoughts made

me sick.

Chapter Three

*"You may not be able to control
what happens to you but you can
control what happens within
you."*

~ Sue Augustine

The following week, my appointment with the therapist went better. I was more at ease because I knew what to expect. The 1980's decor didn't bother me as much anymore, but that smell had to go. When I got to the receptionist's desk, she once again asked for my insurance and ID card. Bingo! I had a current ID card this time, thanks to my visit to the DMV. She was just as nurturing as last time. I liked her. I made a mental note to get her a gift.

I was alone in the waiting room this time, but I didn't care either way. Just like my previous visit, my therapist greeted me at the door and walked me to his office, and this time he was early. I didn't get a chance to use the ladies' room.

"How are you today?" he asked, with a smile.

Just then, I realized I liked him. I could tell that he was a genuine person and cared about the well-being of people. He seemed like the type to volunteer at a soup kitchen or somewhere saving wildlife.

"I'm good," I replied, with an urgency. "Before we get started, here, take this," I said, handing him my homework assignment. "I'll be right back. I really have to go to the ladies' room."

"Oh, go ahead," he responded, getting up to once again to walk me out.

"No, you don't have to; I know where to go."

"Okay, I'll be here when you get back," he said in his genuinely good person tone.

After damn near running to the restroom, I made it! The smell of the cheap perfume was extremely potent in there. It was so bad, I wanted to find their cleaning supplies. I imagined the bottles had 'CHEAP' written across them.

When I returned to the therapist's office, he was in deep concentration, reading my notes. A few minutes after I sat down, he looked up at me. Concern was written all over his face.

"I looked over your notes," he said, looking a little uneasy.

"Okay."

"Living in those conditions had to be hard. I can understand why you're having a lot of built up anger and aggression."

"Actually, I probably do have a lot of aggression built up, but not as much anger. I try not to be one of those 'woe is me' people. I try not to hold on to anger from my past. And most importantly, I'm not (or at least I tell myself), angry with my mother."

"That's good to hear. It isn't safe to carry around anger. That is extremely unhealthy, he replied. Things had to be extremely hard on your grandmother having to take on the responsibility of you and your siblings. I'm sure your mother's addiction left her unable to hold a job. How did that make you feel?"

"My mother would get jobs on and off as a nurse, but they didn't last long. I'm sure they could tell early on that something wasn't right with my mother. When she would go through the interview process, she would make us urinate in a mason jar. This happened several times over the course of the years, but I didn't realize until I was about ten years old that she was using the urine to pass the drug screens. It worked, because she would get the jobs. The jobs only lasted long enough for her to get her first check, and then after that she would come up with different excuses of why she wasn't going back."

"That's the way it normally works when you have an addiction," he said. "That's the only thing that matters."

"You couldn't even imagine unless you witnessed it first-hand. The relationship between an addict and their drug is *all* that matters," I replied.

"You are right," he responded. "I can only imagine. On a better note," he said, trying to break the tension in the room, "I don't think I've ever asked, but, are you married?"

"No, not yet. I'm engaged. My fiancé, Paul, and I were planning on getting married next year, but our plans were postponed."

"Oh, I'm sorry to hear that," he said, concerned.

"Thank you," I replied.

"Why did you ask if I was married?" I asked. "Yes, I know you're trying to get to know me, but your timing seemed suspect," I said, with a smile. "What can you tell about me if I'm married or not?"

"Well," he responded with a chuckle, "I was just trying to get an idea of how your past affected your relationships, if at all."

"My past has had a huge impact on my relationships," I replied. "I had to wear this armor made of steel my entire life and I have yet to figure out how to have it removed. I spent my entire life mastering the art of masking my feelings, and because of this, I am now somewhat emotionless and, at times, unaffectionate. Trying to be in a relationship with a person who is emotionally removed has to be hard. I have a hard time expressing myself and sometimes become evasive, which in turn, makes it hard getting through to me.

"I feel that I'm always being critical and have to be in constant control, and I do not trust anything. This is extremely tiring because I'm always on the edge with everything, not giving myself a chance to relax. My friends and family are often annoyed with my controlling behavior."

"Being this way is totally understandable," he said. "You had to mentally remove yourself from situations on a continuous basis in order to survive. And now that you are in a better place, it isn't easy to just shut that part of you off. As far as the control issues, people often use control as a reaction to the fear of losing control over situations. This often happens when a person experienced abuse in their life. They're so afraid of being vulnerable, that they seek to control their environment in unhealthy ways. How does

Paul deal with this? Does he make you feel guilty for being the way you are?"

"No," I replied. "Paul is a God send. Yes, I'm sure he wishes I was different, but he understands where I came from, and what I've been through. He tells me that I'm a rose that grew from concrete." I said, with a smile. "He knows it's a process."

Chapter Four

"The past is always tense, the future perfect."

~ Zadie Smith ~

School

    Grammar school to me was a blur. I don't remember even going to school in the beginning. My first memory of school was of my mother being so high on the steps that she was sleeping with a plate of egg sandwiches for us. We weren't even concerned with her being there, because we were immune to our situation. We simply grabbed a sandwich and walked out of the door to the bus stop. I don't ever remember doing any homework or projects. My memories of this stage in my life are blocked out.

    In junior high I was extremely insecure because I was an outcast. I didn't have the money like all the other kids to buy the latest fashions or to hang out at the movies, or even go on school field trips. One year I tried out for cheerleading and even made the team, but could not participate because I didn't have the money to buy the cheerleading uniform. I was a gossiper in school, trying to manipulate people into liking me. I would tell them things I heard other people say about them. I was extremely messy.

I was hated by "the popular girls" in school, was an easy target, but was too scared to fight back. One day, a few boys were talking about who they thought were the pretty girls in the classroom. The most popular boy in the classroom said he thought I was pretty. The funny thing was he mentioned several girls' names, but because one name happened to be mine, a big deal was made out of it when the news got back to his girlfriend. That was the worst thing ever. She, along with all her friends, bullied me every day, from that point on. Every day, I was terrified going to school.

Things became so bad that I started carrying a knife to school. I knew it was only a matter of time before those girls jumped me. To avoid the drama, I didn't go to school.

The constant teasing from adolescent girls made me hate school. Being teased about my old, outdated shoes was a weekly occurrence. Luckily, because we wore uniforms every day, my clothes weren't a factor. I wore my natural hair, while all the other girls were already going to the beauty and nail shop. They talked about whatever they could, doing what girls do, but at the time, it was a nightmare. I went to school with the real life 'Mean Girls.'

To escape my reality, I read all the time. I lived through the fantasy on the pages of books. I didn't need anything else; I was content with my books. I would read anything that I could get my hands on. If I wasn't reading, I was writing. Before I was ever touched by a man, I would write short stories and pass them around the classroom for everyone to read about passionate sex-capades between lovers. I used my reading and writing as an escape from the world.

Drinking

When I was twelve years old, I started experimenting with alcohol. I was at my best friend's house, whose mother was a heavy drinker. Her mother noticed our interest in her alcohol, so she gave us some money and told us to go to the store and get some Peach Boone's Farm. I'll never forget it. She wanted to get us drunk so that we could feel the effects of alcohol, hoping that we would never want to drink again. My friend and I drank so much that I was sick for three days, throwing up the entire time. I vowed to never drink again, but that vow was short lived. That was only the beginning. The only thing my friend's mother did was make sure I wouldn't ever drink peach flavored alcohol again. As for everything else, it was bottoms up.

I noticed that alcohol made everything better. When I was down, it would pick me up, and if things were great, alcohol made it greater. Drugs and alcohol became my new norm. I thought that I couldn't have fun unless I was under the influence. My drinking also played a big role in my schooling. I would drink so much that I was too tired or sick to go to school the next day. Even though my mother didn't care, I still made up stories about there being a field trip that I didn't pay for, so they said we could stay home. I could tell that my mother didn't believe my story, but she didn't care either way. The story was really for my granmommy. I didn't want her to be disappointed that I was missing so much school.

My start with men

I feel that my curiosity with sex started so early because, where I grew up, that was the norm. Conversations about sex began as early as I could remember. My fascination with the power women had over men was growing. I watched how my mother was able to feed her habit, thanks to men.

Also, the impression Tina left on me years prior was still strong. I felt that with men, I was liberated, and could be who I was not in school, the shy, timid, unwelcomed school girl. I knew from watching how my mother got what she wanted from men that it would be as easy for me. My curiosity led the way.

****

"You spoke briefly about school in your journal, tell me more."

"We went to several schools, but the first I remember is E.D. White. My sister and I were just having this conversation," I said with a smile. "We must have been the dirtiest children in school because I have vague memories of us jumping out of bed and just leaving out the door." I laughed softly. "I don't remember taking a bath or brushing my teeth. We don't remember our mother combing our hair. I can only imagine what our teachers thought of us. I'm sure we were looked at as the dirty, troubled kids in the class. I hated school so much the smell of school supplies makes me nauseous even today."

"Why do you think this is?"

"Because children are cruel! Not only were we poor, but everyone knew my mother was on drugs. One day, when a new boy came into the classroom that looked a little nerdy, I thought to myself 'hopefully they'll tease him and leave me alone.' I just felt lost all the time. I don't know how I passed every grade, because I did absolutely nothing and learned absolutely nothing. I'm sure we passed because of the pity our teachers had for us.

"By the time I became a teenager and did have control over my schooling, I was too busy living the fast life to care. When I did show up, I just slept in the classroom. I will never forget I had a teacher by the name of Mr. Lindsey who taught me the word, facade. He woke me up from one of my naps and asked me did I know what the word meant. Of course I didn't. He said it's when people put on a front. That's going to be our code word, okay? I cannot have you sleeping in class making me look bad. So when people come in this classroom, put on a facade. I did just that.

"When I was in the 12th grade, I was barely making it to class because I was worn out from living the fast life. At this point I was working at Schwegmann Grocery store and drinking my nights away. I told my father that I did not think that I was going to pass the 12th grade because I had missed too many days. He called the school and informed them that I was homeless and that was why I missed so much school. Because of that, they took pity on me and allowed me to graduate.

"Because I missed more than half the school year that darn Mr. Lindsey protested because they asked him to give me a passing grade. Where most teens would have been upset, I understood. I knew he was looking out for my best interest. Nevertheless, when I heard the news that they were going to allow me to graduate, I was ecstatic!"

"And your drinking?" he asked.

"Well, drinking was just what we did. I was hanging with older people, men especially, so alcohol was always around. I didn't think anything of it. It wasn't an issue, so I thought at the time. I know now that my behavior was destructive, but at the time I didn't care. I used alcohol for every occasion. I used it to have fun or when I needed to drown my sorrows away."

"Do you think the alcohol helped in drowning your sorrows away?"

"Well, at the time it did! Actually," I said with a calmer tone, "even then I knew that my drinking was only numbing how I was feeling, and that's what I needed at the time. I didn't want to feel what I was going through. My lifestyle left me depressed and I was doing what I thought was best."

"You mentioned you have very detailed and vivid dreams. Can we talk about them?"

"Yes, that's fine."

"Tell me about them."

"Well, I always had dreams that I was flying. I was either flying, just to get from point A to point B or I was running from people. Ninety-five percent of my dreams take place at my granmommy's house on O'Reilly Street. I have dreams all the time of my granmommy, people getting killed or raped, my daughter getting raped, dreams about my siblings, and just about everything else you can imagine. I have terrible dreams."

"Tell me the dream about your daughter."

"In one of my dreams, I had my mother babysit her. She was about five years old. Sometime later, my daughter and I were in the bed watching a movie. In the movie, a man and woman were kissing in the bed. When my daughter saw this, she started covering her face and crying. She didn't want to see what was about to happen on the TV. I asked her what was wrong and she just shook her head, crying. She balled her body up in the fetal position and cried, and I just knew. I could tell from her response that someone had done that to her. In my dream I had a vision of what happened to her. In my dream I watched one of my mother's friends with her. I saw everything. I couldn't sleep for weeks afterward. Even now, just talking about it is causing knots in my stomach."

"How are you with your children? Did your past affect your parenting?" he asked.

"Most definitely, it has. I'm a nervous, paranoid wreck behind my children. I am beyond over protective. I constantly worry about everything they do, 24/7. Their safety is top priority to me to the point that I'm smothering them. I do not like for them to spend the night out, so I let all of their friends come over all the time. My son is fourteen and if he's out with his friends, I call him 100 times to make sure he's okay. My daughter has only been allowed to go to one or two sleepovers with her friends and I damn near had diarrhea all night worrying and praying that she was okay. I had to get both of them cell phones to assure constant communication. If we're out and about and I lose sight of them, I feel as though I'm having a panic attack. It's crazy."

"I know you feel it's crazy but it is a natural instinct for parents to be protective over their children. This is where perspective comes into play. What you consider smothering your children, some would think is okay. Do your children ever complain?"

"No. I could be putting too much thought into it, I am kind of obsessive-compulsive sometimes," I responded with a smile.

The therapist chuckled.

"What kind of dreams do you have about your siblings?" he asked.

"The first dream that comes to mind was one where my brother and I were driving down the street. I was the driver and he sat in the passenger seat. We were laughing while stopped at a stop light. Out of nowhere, a man runs up to my side of the car sticking a gun through my window, aiming at my brother. He shot my brother in his face right in front of me. My brother just fell over, hitting his head on the dashboard."

"That had to be very upsetting for you,"

"Very," I replied. "When I awakened from the dream, I was paranoid for weeks. I wondered if I should tell them what I dreamt so that they can watch out, so that it doesn't happen, or do I just keep it to myself? Most of the time I just keep the dreams to myself. Some dreams I can't even bring myself to repeat."

"That is understandable," he replied. "Sometimes it is better to just get them out. If you don't feel up to sharing them with someone, simply write the dream down. That may be a big help to you."

"I will try that next time," I replied.

"What about the men you mentioned in your notes, can you tell me a little about that?"

My whole attitude changed. Suddenly I had a headache.

"I don't mean to be rude, but can we talk about that next time. That's a whole lot of conversation and I'm not in the mood to visit that part of my life right now," I replied.

"Of course we can," he said, worried that he offended me. "No problem," he reassured. "Are you okay?"

"Yes, I'm fine. I just didn't prepare myself mentally to take that particular journey down memory lane."

"That's totally understandable," he says. "How about you write about it and I can read it during our next visit."

"Okay, I can do that."

"I understand that some people are more comfortable writing about their experiences in detail rather than talking about it in detail."

"I can write, that's no problem. I just don't want you thinking I'm another Karrine Steffans."

"Who?"

"Never mind," I answered with a chuckle, knowing he didn't have a clue.

Chapter Five

*"If it wasn't for the rain, flowers
wouldn't grow."*

~Daniel Winston~

First Time

My first time was extremely memorable. Not because it was a beautiful experience, but rather, quite the contrary. When I was twelve years old I went to spend the night at my best friend Nia's house. Nia and I were inseparable. We did everything together. I loved her and her mother. Their house was my home away from home. Nia's mother taught me things that I still hold dear today. Nia's mother had a drinking problem, but I didn't care. It wasn't as bad as my mother's drug addiction, so being at their house made me feel safe. When we got to her house her mother's boyfriend's nephew was there. His name was Sean. They were all drinking and hanging out, just having a good time. Her mother introduced us, and right away I thought he was the most beautiful person on earth.

I guess when I walked away he made a funny comment or looked at me a certain way because I heard Nia's mother saying, "Oh no!

Don't mess with her! She's like my daughter."

Right away I froze with excitement. He likes me?

Little ole me? Little ole skinny, non-developed me?

I never knew the value that I held. I was just

amazed that he wanted me. I heard her telling him

"You are way too old for her. You're about 22,

right?" I couldn't hear his response, but that was

okay. I had heard enough.

A few minutes later, Sean came in the back

where we were and told me to write down his phone

number. He told me to call him later that night. I

was so excited, and felt so honored. I couldn't stop

smiling.

The first night that I met him, the first night

that I saw his face, when Nia's mother went to

sleep, I snuck out of the house with him.

He was driving an older modeled car that he

recently had painted purple. He bragged on how it

was supposed to be orange, but the guy messed up.

He told me that it was going to be repainted the

following week. I didn't care if the car was the color
of a rainbow, as long as I was in it.

The smell of his cologne along with the car
freshener he used was intoxicating. He had me sit
right next to him while he drove. Nervous, scared,
and not knowing what to think, I did as he asked.
Next, he put his arm around my waist. I thought he
was being so romantic. I was so flattered by this
gesture. What he did next I didn't expect. He put
his hand in my panties. I was in shock, utter shock,
but I allowed it. Right there in the car, he started
fondling me. I was in such shock by what was
happening I didn't know how to react. I just stared
out of the window, not knowing how I was
supposed to act or feel.

That night we didn't go anywhere to get to
know each other and talk. We didn't go anywhere to
get something to eat. We went right to his place.

When I walked in, I saw female belongings
and children's toys everywhere. He told me that he

and his girlfriend had broken up and he'd thrown her and their kids out. Not knowing how to feel about this, I tried not to think about it.

Looking around, I noticed roaches everywhere. I guess he noticed as well. He mumbled something about telling her to buy roach spray, but obviously she didn't. He took me into the bedroom which was only big enough for a bed and a TV stand. He turned on the radio that was at the bottom of the TV stand and R. Kelly's "Seems Like You're Ready" was playing on the radio. He looked at me and asked, "Are you ready?" I thought, 'Ready for what?' He sat me down on the bed and took off my clothes, and right there, on a mattress with no sheets, I gave my virginity to a man I'd met a few hours earlier. Afterwards, while we got dressed, he got a call. It must have been one of his customers, because he pulled out his stash and bagged his product. I guess he was trying to impress me, because he did all of this in front of me, and it worked. Drugs weren't new to me, but being with the drug dealer instead of the drug addict was exciting.

From that day on, I was in awe, I was in love, and would do anything for that man, anything that made him happy.

When I finally went home after spending a few days at Nia's house, my mother overheard me on the phone talking about my experience with one of my friends. I was in the kitchen talking away, not paying attention to the fact my mother was standing in the doorway. When I noticed her, she went crazy. She called Nia and her mother over to my granmommy's house to get to the bottom of everything. I told her they didn't know anything about it (I lied), but since I was at their house she called them anyway. Before they came over I talked to Sean on the phone to inform him of what was happening and he told me to go to the store and get a douche to wash away his fluids. I did.

After the meeting was held, we went to the hospital so that a rape kit could be used. I told them that I douched and that the act happened several days ago, but they still went through with everything. When they told me that they were going to keep my panties, I asked them, "What do you expect to find? It happened days ago and I already douched." The doctor asked if Sean ejaculated inside me. I had no clue what he was talking about. I was so young and so naive.

I wondered why my mother even cared. She never cared before now. I felt she made a big deal because she thought that was what she was supposed to do; that's what a caring mother would do.

Nothing was ever done to Sean. I protected him because I loved him (after knowing him less than a week). I told everyone that I came in contact with that he did not rape me.

It didn't hurt that he was a drug dealer and my mother was a drug addict. In her eyes, we were a match made in heaven. So there we were, a twelve-year old Christian with a 22-year-old drug dealing man.

Player... or so I thought

Now that I'd experienced what all the fuss was about when it came to sex, I started to use this to my advantage. My father had a lady friend named Tammy who lived in a suburb of New Orleans. Ava and I used to visit her quite often. Tammy loved our father and wanted to get us out of our situation as often as possible. She would give our mother drugs in order to let us go, and it worked. Tammy had several older children that we loved to hang with. One of her sons had a friend named Adam, who liked me. Adam and I became friends, and later, I became his girlfriend. Although it all happened so fast, once again, I thought I was in love. One night, while drinking and partying,

*one thing led to another and I gave him my
virginity (so he thought). I was too embarrassed for
him to know that I already had sex at twelve, so I
made him think he was my first. I had my grown
man back home plus my little boyfriend in the
suburbs. I thought that I was a player.*

*My fast ways soon got the best of me. I
thought I was being a player, but the joke was on
me. One night, a friend of Tammy's family, who
had to be about 30 years old, came over to the house.
He had a dark complexion and had to be about 6'3,
weighing 200 pounds. I was asleep on the bed and
he was lying on the floor in front of me watching
TV. He took my hand and started sucking on my
fingers. I felt what was going on, but was still half
asleep, so I thought I was dreaming. He got on top
of me while I was sleeping. What woke me up was
feeling his penis entering inside me. I wondered
what the hell was going on? I was too scared to
scream. I thought if I said anything that he was*

going to tell Tammy that I was having sex with Adam or he would beat me. When he was done, he left me there and went back to whatever he was doing. I thought I deserved it for some reason. I didn't tell anyone but my sister and what she said next, blew me away. She said that he had done the same thing to her. We never told anyone.

Everyone has a Price

One of the hardest memories that I had to face was the fact that my mother sold her daughters to the highest bidder. We were children, and because we had no guidance, we were out in the streets, attracting all kinds of men. My mother would allow us to date whoever we wanted, no matter how old he was, as long as they provided her with drugs. My sister and I have vivid memories of her making guys we were interested in, or even guys that showed interest in us, buy her drugs in order to receive her approval.

My sister remembered one day when a guy came to see her without drugs to give my mother. My mother and the boy drove around to different neighborhoods looking for drugs. Embarrassed by what was happening, my sister asked could they take her home, but my mother refused until they found what they were looking for. Once they found her drugs, my mother allowed my sister and the guys to go on their merry way. There was even talk that my mother performed sexual favors for money with some of the guys that we were dating. I'm not sure how true this was, but I didn't doubt it.

Jodie's Dad

As time went on, I continued going to school and hanging with my friends. Other than Nia, Jodie was a really close friend of mine. One day when I was about thirteen, my friends and I decided to cut school and go over to Jodie's house. Being the mischievous girls that we were, we decided to watch some of her parents' porn in their bedroom.

Everything was going smoothly the entire morning until just before noon when we were caught by her dad. Her dad was an older man who had one regular leg and one prosthetic. He was the kind of man who always looked dirty because of the type of work he did. When he noticed that we were scared, right away he said, "It's okay, I don't mind you girls being here." Instead of him getting mad at us, he encouraged us to continue watching the porn, saying that we had to learn. He also told us which videos he thought were the best.

He even told us the story about the time he was having sex and the woman squirted on him. Our naive reactions were "EWW, that's gross!" We teased him and said that she urinated on him. He went on explaining to us what squirting meant. To make sure we didn't have to stop for a lunch break, he even took our orders and went out and bought us Rally's hamburgers. We knew that this was totally

bizarre and inappropriate behavior on his behalf,
but we were so ignorant at the time, we didn't care.

Our daily routine continued without
missing a beat. I would walk to her house every
morning and we would walk to school together. One
day when I arrived to her house her dad was outside
working on his truck. When he saw me, he smiled. I
asked him why he was smiling. He told me that he
was in love. I responded, "Oh, that's great!" He
said, "You don't understand. I'm in love with you."
I didn't know what to say, so I didn't say anything.
As time went on, every time her dad saw me he
made advances towards me. I knew that he was
serious because he molested his daughters as well.
He offered me rides if he saw me at the bus stop and
gave me money, just because. I knew that he wanted
me and to impress me he was going to pay up. I took
advantage of his kindness and took what he had to
give. One day my friend asked me if he had ever
tried anything with me because he was looking at

*me the same way he looked at her. I couldn't bring
myself to tell the truth.*

Kirk

*One day my friends and I were talking
about sex during our lunch break at school. A friend
named Tanya showed up and told us we should
come and hang with her at her Uncle Kirk's house.
She told us how good their sex was and that he had
asked her to find more girls for him. Not thinking
anything of it, and not having a care in the world,
we made plans for the weekend and went with her.*

*Kirk came and picked all of us up and took
us to his house. Once again being ignorant to the
situation, we didn't consider the inappropriateness
of this man being Tanya's uncle. As it turned out,
he was married to Tanya's aunt. After laughing at
Tanya about how trifling she was for having sex
with her aunt's husband, we didn't think any more
of it.*

He gave us drugs and alcohol to loosen us up as soon as we got in the car. We were all drunk and high out of our minds. When we got to his house, before we knew it, one big orgy was going on. I don't even remember the specifics because I was out of it most of the time. But I do remember coming in and out of it to find him doing something sexual to me or one of the other girls who were in the bed with us. We were about fourteen and Kirk was 37. I guess we left some of our belongings there because his wife found out and called my mother. When my mother found out, she was too high to care. The lady told her that she should take me to get tested because her husband was a whore. My mother simply listened to what the woman on the phone had to say and her response was "okay."

When she hung up the phone, she neither screamed nor hit me, as I expected. But what she did say, I will never forget. She told me if I was out fucking and sucking dick, I should at least get paid for it. Those were the only words of wisdom I'd ever received from my mom.

Correction, she gave me words of wisdom on one other occasion. She told me about a trip she took to Las Vegas with her friends. She told me when they spent all of their money that they each called their boyfriends and told them they were pregnant and needed an emergency abortion. They needed the guys to send them the money to pay for it. These funds paid for the remainder of their vacation. She told me this, so, in case of an emergency, I had a sure way to get some money. I guess these were her survival tips. Every so often she would ask for money, and if I didn't have it she would say, "Remember what I said about my Vegas trip."

Norm
One night I was at this bar with one of my friends when this guy approached me. He whispered

in my ear, asking if I wanted to make the money
that was in his pocket. Me, being the dumb ass that
I was, said yes. When we got to the door, I saw
another guy outside that I was dealing with, so at
the last minute, I didn't go. I went and got my
friend and told her to go with him instead. Without
question, she did. When she returned, we split the
profits. This kind of activity became my norm. I had
to do whatever it took.

In the Streets
I put myself in harm's way all the time.
Following behind Sean, I was always in the streets.
One night when I was about fifteen, he and I were
at his sister's house and we had an argument. I
became upset, left the house, and walked to the bus
stop to go home. It was probably about 10:30pm.
When I got to the bus stop, a white van pulled up
with about four guys in it. The guy who was in the
front passenger seat was talking to me, but at the

same time, the driver was talking into his ear. I heard him say "get her." The passenger was still talking to me as he was shaking his head, okay, to "get her." He started to open the door as he tied a white bandanna around his fist. When I saw this, I took off screaming and running. I felt his fingertips brush my shoulder as he tried to grab me. Luckily for me, the house across the street had people on their porch and I had a place to run. At this time, in New Orleans, girls were getting snatched, raped, and robbed. After calming down, I went back to Sean's sister's house and told him what happened. Being the street hoodlum he was, he grabbed his gun and he and I walked down the street looking for the van. I felt so safe and honored because my man had my back. Boy, was I oblivious to reality.

After that night, I had dreams about being kidnapped and held prisoner. Instead of getting away, they caught me and kept me in the back of the van. To make sure nobody saw me, they made me lay down the entire time. I couldn't even lift my head. They just kept me there as they drove around the city.

Trying to survive

I was a teenager doing what I thought I had to do, just to survive. I had so many men I kept around because I needed what they had, money. My mother taught me early on what I had to do to get what I needed. I was pretty much living the life of an adult and put myself in harm's way on numerous occasions. I didn't have parents to support me and I wouldn't dare ask my granmommy for anything. I would put money in her wallet without her knowing, to help out around the house. I didn't know a better way. I was one lost soul, often left not knowing how to feel. I didn't know what was normal anymore. I just went with the flow of everything that was thrown my way.

I had a nervous breakdown when I was sixteen. I didn't know at the time what was happening to me, but thought that I was being rebellious. I wanted to do something, anything, that wasn't the norm. I felt different from my peers and I wanted to look the part. One day I went over to my friend Faye's house, who used to do our hair. When I sat in the chair she asked me what kind of style I wanted. I told her to cut off all of my hair. I noticed she was taking forever to get started, doing everything but my hair. When I asked her what was wrong, she told me that she did not want to cut it. She hesitated, hoping I would change my mind. I told her it was fine, do it or I would cut it myself. When she saw I was serious she said "Okay, I'll do it!" She cut off my long ponytail and handed it to me. This was only the start. At that moment I felt free.

My hair being cut off still wasn't enough. I wanted more. I wanted to rebel against everything normal. I thought, "Ain't shit else about me normal, may as well not look it." Around the same time, I became interested in tattoos. Sean and I went to the tattoo parlor together and he convinced me get his name tattooed on me. The tattoo artist, which was a customer of mine from a grocery where I worked, told me that despite my age, he would tattoo me. He heard the conversation that was going on between Sean and me (him telling me to get his name) and told me that he could refuse to do my tattoo if I wanted. He said that he could tell that I was reluctant and didn't want me to regret getting the tattoo later. I knew deep down inside that I was going to regret it, but I did it anyway. In a matter of a week I went back and received three more huge tattoos. These tattoos are probably the only thing I regret about my life. These tattoos remind me every day of how naive and dumb I once was.

I used my body as a way to get back at the world, because that was all I had control over. I

needed to feel like I had control over something,
anything, so I used my body. No one could tell me
what to do with my body, so I did with it as I
pleased. And the more something was looked upon
as being 'bad' the bigger rush it gave me.

****

"After reading your notes I understand why you didn't want to talk about this chapter in your life during our last visit. I'm sure these experiences had to be hard for you. When you look back on this today, how do you feel? How do you think you were affected by everything you experienced?" the therapist asked.

"I don't think that I was affected," I replied. "Well, let me rephrase this. I *know* that I was affected in some way or another, but in what way, I'm not sure. I know that my past played a big role in my emotional makeup. As far as romantically, I don't know. I do not have any hang-ups when it comes to sex, if you're wondering. I don't know how to explain it, but like I mentioned before, things do not affect me like they do others."

"I have a question. How important is sex to you today? When you look back on all you've done, do you feel any regret? Do you feel any shame? Do you have any sexual dysfunction? For example, if a woman is raped, sometimes the memory of this affects her ability to have a normal sex life."

"I see where you are coming from," I replied. "When you put it like that, I guess I do have issues in the sex department. In my opinion, sex was no big deal, and that can be an issue. Sex didn't have the significance to me that it should have. I guess I never knew my self-worth enough to save myself until the right time. I was just having fun, when in reality, I knew better. I knew that I was being used as an object, but I convinced myself that I didn't care, as long as I got what I wanted."

"What are your thoughts about sex now? Does it hold any significance?" he asked.

"Yes, most definitely. I know now that sex isn't a tool to get what I want. It actually has meaning now. That's one of the things that I loved about my fiancé. Our relationship wasn't based around sex. He wanted to know me further than the physical. He wanted to know what I had between my ears. He was the first man to ever ask me about my thoughts and desires."

"You speak very highly about your fiancé. He must be a good guy."

"Yes, he is."

Chapter Six

*"Never let the past spoil your
present or govern your future."*

~ Author Unknown ~

Olympus Has Fallen

When I was about seventeen years old, my granmommy could no longer keep her house. The bills became too much and she was entirely too old to continue working as a nursing assistant. She had to sell it. I was devastated when she told me, and felt lost. That house was all I'd known. It was my only source of security. I went through a deep depression. I didn't know what I was going to do. When she sold it, I felt empty, like my security blanket was taken away. All of my memories, both good and bad, happened in that house.

I started to really lose it around this time. I was like a zombie. I was physically present, but my mind was somewhere else. I was drinking more than ever and my behavior became more reckless than before. I went through a whirlwind of emotions. Sadness, hopelessness, and an overbearing feeling of being alone overcame me. All I could do was cry. I cried for my family. Why was this happening to us?

My granmommy took the profits from the house and gave $10,000 to my mother and $10,000 to my uncle, and she moved into a retirement building in New Orleans East. My mother took some of her money and rented a little house around the corner from where we used to live. Ava and Joel were in Chicago with our father and Misty was living on her own with my nephew, so that left Kenan and me.

I couldn't live with my mother. I could no longer stand the drugs and all the different men coming in and out. I did not trust the situation. I didn't feel safe with her. I told Sean that my granmommy was selling her house and he rented us a little apartment to share.

I went to my mother's house on several occasions. When things became unbearable with Sean, I even tried to live with her for a little while. I just couldn't stand the living conditions. She kept the house just like all the others - filthy. The drug use and men going in and out were at an all-time high. The situation was so bad that I preferred the hostile situation I was in instead of living with my mother.

My last memory of the house was when my mother was being evicted. Although my granmommy gave her $10,000, she only paid three month's rent. The owners took all of her belongings and put them on the street. I could remember wanting to help her as the local crack heads started taking a few of her things and the wind blew away things such as papers and pictures. She and Sean were not on good terms, from something drug related, so he pulled me by the arm and said, "Come on, let's go. This isn't our problem." I was so emotionally drained, I had no fight left inside. He threw me in the car like a rag doll. I could remember feeling guilt in the pit of my stomach as we drove away. At that moment I felt as though I had to fix my mother's problem. I wished so badly, at that *moment, that our dysfunctional family was back*

together. Yes, we were messed up, but at least we

were all together. I worried about what would

happen to my mother. How would she survive

alone?

We went back to that dump we shared and I

drank my sorrows away.

All of this happened so long, ago, yet I

remember it like it was yesterday. A part of me died

during that time in my life.

No longer having anywhere to live, my

mother found one of her male friends who was a

trucker and left town with him. She told my

brother, Kenan, that he was a boy and that he could

survive on his own. He ended up living with one of

his friends for a little while.

I emailed the therapist my notes so that
he could read over them before our session. I
didn't want to see his facial reactions as he
read my truth. I was positive he had never met

a person like me. I don't know why, but I was concerned about what he thought of me. I could tell he grew up in a world way different than mine.

"Hello, Christian," he greeted me with a smile, gesturing for me to walk with him to his office.

"Hi," I replied, a little shy and uneasy because I knew he'd read my notes.

"How have you been?"

"I've been good."

"Well, as you probably already know, I read the notes you sent me."

"Yes," I replied, faintly.

"You mentioned before in one of our sessions that you have an issue with control. Reading your notes, this is understandable. During your entire life you didn't have control over anything, and because of this you were left feeling helpless when you saw it fall apart.

You didn't have control over your grandmother losing her house, you didn't have control over your mother and her drug abuse, and you were taken advantage of sexually. Now that you're an adult, and you are able to control your surroundings, you do just that, control them. This isn't always a bad thing."

"It is in my relationship, when I can't let my man be the man, or when my children aren't in my eyesight and I feel like I'm going to have a panic attack. I need to learn how to relax. I do not always want to be in control, or feel that I have to be. I want to be able to trust with a clear mind. I want to be able to let go without secretly checking to making sure everything is going as expected."

"Your actions are understandable and I need you to understand this. It is my opinion that you developed this need to be in control because your parents were emotionally unavailable when you were growing up and your environment was not stable. When a person experienced or is experiencing emotional or physical instabilities and has no choice in the matter, they sometimes attempt to control other parts of their lives and in many cases, they overdo it, becoming controlling. I feel as though you are trying to protect a part of you that was hurt many years ago. What we have to do is find ways to help you cope better with your actions. We have to find ways to help you deal with this need for control without feeling the need to act upon it."

I agreed, feeling relieved that I wasn't as crazy as I thought.

Chapter Seven

"Rain doesn't last forever."

~ Author Unknown ~

Sean

    Sean was my first. We started off when I was twelve and he was 22 years old. Although our start was bumpy, with my mother finding out and all, it didn't end there. At first, we were sneaking around so my granmommy wouldn't know we were together, but after a while, everyone knew. Sean was my main boyfriend. The other men were used when I needed them.

    I think the mental abuse I sustained while with Sean was just as bad, if not worse, as having a drug addicted mother. It was like I left one abusive situation and went right into another.

    Throughout our entire relationship, Sean had other women. He even had children with other women. I would find out about them when he told me we had to go get checked for STD's or when one of them became pregnant. Dealing with this type of dysfunction was bad enough for an adult, but putting a child through this was traumatizing. I thought I was in love, so whenever something came up (women), to make myself feel better about the situation, I turned to other men. In my little immature mind, this was payback for what he was doing to me. Did it make me feel better or vindicated? No, but I needed to tell myself it did to justify continuing our relationship.

I was so brainwashed by Sean that I would do anything he asked. I gave him my entire paycheck from my little rinky dink jobs. He even had me have sex with his friends. I was always out in the streets with him while he conducted his petty drug dealer business. I've witnessed and have gone through some of the craziest things in my life. I thought we were going to get killed one day in those streets. I justified possibly dying by telling myself, at least I would die with the man I loved.

I purposely became pregnant with Sean's baby, thinking that would bring us closer, but I had two miscarriages. I remember picking Sean up from jail, knowing about all the violent crimes he'd committed, but too scared to tell a soul. I thought I was going to go crazy having to hold all of this on my teenage shoulders.

We fought all the time, yes, actual physical fights. Sean was extremely jealous and questioned every move I made. He would get mad if I took a shower after we had sex. He said it didn't matter if I smelled like sex to everyone else. Who did I need to smell fresh for? I had to sneak and wash up or wait until he left to bathe, in order to prevent a fight. One particular fight I remember in detail was him coming over to my mother's house to get me because I went there alone. Something as innocent as me wanting to visit my mother turned into an all-out war. The tongue lashing that he gave me, calling me every hoe and bitch in the book wasn't enough, so he became physical. He grabbed me by my neck, choking me. My mother jumped on his back, trying to pull him off of me while crying and screaming,

begging for him to let me go. I remember thinking
that he was going to kill me that day. I also
remember wishing he had.

Sean would even come up to my school to
argue and fight. On one particular day, the
principal was coming into the school and just
watched while shaking his head. I thought, 'Really?
You're not going to help me?' Sean would put
hickeys all over my neck before I went to school,
telling me he was doing it so no one else would
want me.

I remember a time when we were fighting
while he was driving. I wanted to get my hair done
and because he did not know the beautician (I must
have been having sex with the beautician), he
wouldn't allow it. He took all of my hair products
that I'd bought and threw them out of the window.
He then started punching me like I was a punching
bag. At this point, I was tired of being beat and
fought back. I laid back on the passenger seat of the

car and begun kicking him in the face. I envisioned
kicking his head off of his body, but settled on the
idea of kicking him out of the car. With every kick I
released built up aggression and hate. At this point
the car was swerving out of control. I didn't care.
His friend was in the back seat and instead of him
telling him not to hit me, he just took the wheel of
the car from the back seat, while we fought.

When we moved in together, I felt like a
prisoner and Sean was my captor. He now had the
upper hand because I had to rely on him for shelter.
I no longer had any freedom and no say so about
anything. I had to ask for permission for everything.
One day my friend asked me to come to her house
and babysit. Of course, I had to ask Sean. He told
me no (because I must be having sex with her).
When I told her, she understood without making me
feel stupid.

He even had a tape recorder that he hooked up to the phone. He listened in on all of my phone conversations.

I could remember feeling like I would die behind some of Sean's actions. At that point, I hated men, I hated Sean, and I hated myself. I hated the life that I was living.

This relationship scarred me for every other relationship to come. My self-esteem, self-respect, and any self-worth were at an all-time low. I was mentally and physically broken down to the core. The words I'm writing to explain the anguish I suffered while in this relationship can't begin to make anyone understand what I went through. I stayed in this abusive relationship five years. I strongly believe that that relationship helped mold me negatively into the person I am today.

Free

When I got home from work one night, I received a call from Sean's sister. She told me that he had been arrested and the severity of his charges meant that he was going to be there for awhile. When she told me that, a rush came over me and I almost fell to the floor. The feelings were a mixture of guilt and happiness. Guilt, because I was excited over another person's pain, and happy, because I was finally free.

I knew that I couldn't stay in that house. In New Orleans, people's doors were kicked in all the time. Once word got out that he was in jail, I knew my door would be next.

I didn't know what to do, because I didn't have anywhere to go. For the next few nights, I stayed with random men, drinking and doing drugs, just to have somewhere to lay my head. I would go back to that dump where I lived early in the morning just to change clothes, thinking, 'They

*won't kick in the door while it's morning,' and
would leave right back out. I was scared out of my
mind.*

*When I was tired of living from pillar to
post, I called my friend, Faye, and told her my
situation. She welcomed me to stay at her house
with open arms. I also called my father. We agreed
that after graduation I would go back to Chicago
with him. Everything was falling into place. I
finally wore a genuine smile.*

Scared Straight (well, not really)

*That night, I packed a bag and caught the
bus to Faye's house. When I got off of the bus and
started walking to her house, this guy driving down
the street stopped to talk to me. He asked me did I
want to go and get something to eat. I thought,
'Sure, why not?' I wanted to celebrate my new
found freedom. I had him bring me to Faye's to drop
off my things and then we were off. He had alcohol*

with him that we drank straight from the bottle. I

didn't even know what was in the bottle and

honestly, I didn't care. I couldn't even tell you what

the guy looked like, because it was so dark. I didn't

care, I was free! We were in his car, talking and

drinking until I noticed that we were driving kind

of far out. I asked him where were we going? He

said, to his house. I didn't think anything of it. I

was so reckless; I was used to this. When we got to

his house he went over to the dresser and formed

three lines of heroin on the dresser. He did two lines

and asked me if I wanted the third. I didn't. He

hunched his shoulders like, oh well, and did the line

himself. A few minutes later his whole demeanor

changed. He came over to me and said "You know I

could kill you, right?" I thought to myself, just

when I got myself out of one messed up situation,

here I go getting in another. I told him "Yeah, I

know," trying to remain calm. The entire time I'm

thinking to myself 'What the FUCK! Like,

REALLY, Christian? REALLY?' The usual fright most people would have experienced was nowhere to be found, but instead I was pissed at myself for getting into this situation. He ordered me to take off my clothes. I did. He had sex with me, and when he was done, he took me back to Faye's like nothing ever happened. I was so happy to get home safely that I didn't care what he did to my body. Sex was just a meaningless interaction to me. What he did to me was nothing.

At this point, sex, drugs, and alcohol were everywhere. I couldn't escape them, no matter where I went, and at that point, I was grateful for that. When I went to live with Faye, I met her boyfriend, Parker. Parker was a nice man, and I remember thinking that he wasn't bad looking to be in his forties. Although he did not live with Faye, he was there quite often. We would hang out, play cards and watch movies. I felt welcome. Even though they were older than me, they made me feel a

part of their little circle by including me. One day,
Faye came to me saying that she wanted to ask me
for a favor. Shocking the hell out of me, she said
Parker wanted to have a threesome with she and I.
Don't get me wrong, at this stage in my life sex was
no biggie, and my mentality was already so screwed
up that being with a girl was just like being with a
man, but I cared for my friend and I didn't want to
do anything that would hurt her relationship. I told
her I didn't want to do it. She pleaded with me
because he was helping her pay her bills and she
wanted to make him happy. I told her that I would
not have sex with him, but we could give him a
show. I told her she and I could have sex, but he
could only watch. She was happy with that.

The next morning, I was so drunk from our
festivities that I was passed out on the living room
floor (I do not know how I got there). Faye was at
work, so this left Parker and me alone. The minute I
heard the door close, he started trying to wake me

up to have sex. I told him to leave me alone, but he did not. He continued to feel all over me and picked me up and put me on the sofa. I started screaming and crying at this point for him to leave me alone. I couldn't believe this fool was trying to make me have sex. Was he really trying to rape his girlfriend's friend? When he wouldn't listen to my cries, thinking quick, trying to get myself out of this situation, I made a deal with him. I promised him that we could have a threesome before I left for Chicago. I made up some story about not wanting to do anything behind Faye's back. With these words, he left me alone. I fell back to sleep, with my last thoughts being, I couldn't wait to get to Chicago.

I called Faye while she was at work and told her what happened. I was extremely grateful for our friendship and her being there for me when I was in need. I told her that I would never do anything with Parker, and out of respect, she should know of his actions. She asked me what she should do, because he paid her bills. I told her to do nothing. Let him continue to pay her.

Needless to say, I didn't have any intentions on having a threesome. I left for Chicago and never looked back.

Chapter Eight

"Forget the past."

~ Nelson Mandela ~

My move to Chicago

Just like we planned, after my graduation from high school, my brother Kenan and I moved to Chicago. At that point, I was so relieved that I no longer had to handle all the weights of the world by myself. When my father came to pick us up, I felt great. I no longer had to wonder where I was going to live and how was I was going to get by. I no longer had to feel like a prisoner and fear for my life. I could be normal and put my old life behind me.

I felt like I had a second chance at life.

The first thing I wanted to do when I got to Chicago was enroll in school, and I did. I enrolled at Olive Harvey College, but things did not go as I expected. Being there felt just like school felt before. I felt lost. I tried my best to understand, but it was to no avail. My mental state wasn't ready to take on a challenge so extensive.

My time at Olive Harvey was short lived, because not long after arriving to Chicago, I became pregnant. When I was about seven months along, I stopped going to school.

I was nineteen years old when I had my son, Daniel.

Shortly after having my son, we moved from Chicago to Naperville. When my son was a year old, I was sitting with him on the sofa watching TV at my dad's house. I was already feeling like a loser because I had dropped out of school and needed to do something with my life. I saw a Robert Morris College commercial and I called. Within no time, I was enrolled.

I can honestly say that my experience at RMC was great. The classes were small, so I was able to get the one on one attention I needed. I couldn't believe the same girl who barely made it to class in the past, was there every day, hours early, studying in the lab. Every semester I made the Principal's Honors, except for the last. I loved school at that point. I loved learning. I loved being a part of something big.

The old Christian was up to her old habits. While in school, I wasn't working, so that hustle mentality kicked in. I can honestly say that I had twelve guys I was dealing with that I kept at arm's reach. I had twelve different guys that I slept with, on and off. I remembered this number because I would laugh, saying that I had a basketball team worth of men at my disposal. I thought this was something to brag about.

While in school my friends would tell me that I was living better than they were, as they admired my things. They were working, yet I had no job. I would just look at them and smile. I knew what they were alluding to, but I didn't confirm their suspicions. I didn't want anyone to know how I got my money. I didn't want them to look at me like so many had when I lived in New Orleans. I looked like this nice little innocent girl and that's how I liked it. I even befriended personnel in school if my classes became too challenging. One thing would lead to another, and I would have my A. I was happy that I was able to maintain my GPA without a care about the cost. My closest friend caught on to my hustle real fast. This caused me to lose our friendship, because she didn't approve. This didn't stop me, though. That was all I knew.

After finishing school and finding a job in my profession, I still attempted to fill a void by dealing with men. I convinced myself that I was only having fun. I constantly made excuses for my actions.

Once again, because of my fast ways, I ended up pregnant at 24 years old. This time with my daughter, McKenzie

Chapter Nine

"Death leaves a heartache no one can heal,

Love leaves a memory no one can steal."

~ Author Unknown ~

Goodbye

My granmommy passed away on February 23, 2007. When she passed, I was heartbroken. I loved my granmommy with all of my heart. God took the most pure, loving person that had ever walked on earth. Did I blame Him? If I was Him, I would have wanted her by my side as well.

Mom

After living in Chicago some time, my mother came to live there as well. She lived with distant family members. While there, another family member became ill, and they needed someone to take care of him. My mother being a nurse, and needing a place to live, the situation seemed ideal. I was happy that my mother was in Chicago with us. I was hoping to have a second chance with her. I wanted my children to have a relationship with their grandmother. I had always envied the mother-daughter relationships I saw in other families while simultaneously longing for one of my own. I had always wished I had a mother that I could go to for advice about life, a mother I could look up to, and a mother I could count on.

My mother seemed to be getting her life together. I was extremely hopeful for her and thought that the change in scenery could be her second chance at life.

Right before I had my daughter, we moved closer to my mother, with the hopes of starting over so that I could finally have the relationship I desperately needed. I wanted to make peace with my mother. I did not want to feel any harsh feelings toward her like I had my entire life.

Boy! Was that one of the biggest mistakes ever. I felt like I was reliving my childhood all over again.

My mother wasn't getting her life together. In fact, she was still the same drug addict she'd been my entire life. My mother continually harassed me for money. Now it was worse, because I had a job.

There were times that she would come to my house at 2:00am or 3:00am, begging for money. She was already desperate, which made her violent, so I would give her the money just to make her leave.

Just like when we were growing up, everyone knew my mother was a drug addict. She was, once again, the token hype of the neighborhood. Whenever she did anything wrong to support her habit such as steal or cheat someone out of their money, I would get that knock on the door from other drug addicts she hung out with to inform me. Because my mother and I looked just alike, everywhere I went, other random drug addicts would shout out, "HEY! ARE YOU SAUNDRA'S DAUGHTER?" The only difference this time was that I was an adult and didn't care.

One of the most embarrassing days of my life happened when a few friends and I went out for a girl's night. Not ready to go in, we decided to go out for an early breakfast. It had to be about 3:00am.

On our way home, I saw about five people walking down the street. As we got closer they were laughing loud and carrying on in the middle of the street, so it caught our attention. It was a bunch of drug addicts, obviously high in their own little world, having a good old time, with my mother as the ring leader.

I loved my mother dearly. Through everything she put me and my family through, my love never wavered. Because of the love I had for my mother, I could remember wishing that she was dead, not because she was an awful person, but because if I knew she was dead, at least I knew she would be safe.

"How did things work with her living with her uncle? Did he know about her drug use?" asked the therapist.

"I'm sure he knew of her drug use. Things didn't work out with them. I'm not sure exactly how it happened, but they found out she was abusing him. Not only was she physically abusive, but she also took all of his money. None of his bills were being paid and she even took the money he needed for his medication. Because he wasn't taking his medication, he ended up in the hospital. I was told because he only had one bedroom, my mother made him sleep in his chair while she shared his bed with different men. When all of this came to light, they made her leave. She moved into a low income building a few miles away."

"Did you see her often once she moved?" he asked.

"No, not really. When I did see her a few months later, her front teeth were missing. She said she had an accident, but I knew better. If the wear and tear of the drug use did not do it, then someone knocked them out."

"How is your mother doing now?"

"In 2008 my mother died of drug related causes."

"I'm sorry to hear that," he replied.

"Thank you."

"Do you mind if we talk about it?"

"I don't mind," I replied. "When I found out about my mother's death, I was on my way to work. I received a call. The man on the other line said 'Baby, I'm sorry but your momma is dead.' Just like that. No emotion, just very matter of fact."

"Oh, really?" the therapist responded, in shock.

"Yes," I replied. "I immediately called the building where she was living to see if he was telling the truth. It turned out, he was. The woman on the line asked me to come to the building. She also had no emotion. She made it seem as though I had to come to the building right then and there.

"I figured she needed me to come to the building to sign some papers in order to release the apartment. When I got there, the lady told me to go to my mother's apartment. Not thinking anything of it, I did. When I got to my mother's floor there was a policeman coming out of her apartment. When he saw that I was coming to the apartment he asked me was I ready. Still ignorant of the situation I told him, yes, and went into the apartment.

"Next, was one of the hardest things to witness. My mother was still lying in her bed, lifeless. The room was somber. She had to have been there for a couple of days because rigor mortis already started. Her skin was grey and she released her bowels all over her white night gown. I'm not sure if she threw up or if she was foaming from the drugs but some type of substance was coming out her mouth. All of her drug paraphernalia was laid out neatly on the table in front of the bed, next to about five different empty prescription medication bottles that didn't belong to her.

"The smell of her decaying body was heavy in the air. It was unbearable. I witnessed all of this with no warning whatsoever, and at that moment a plethora of emotions took over. It was all entirely too much to handle. I lost it. That's when I saw her. I saw the lost little girl I kept hidden away in the back of my mind show herself. It was like an out of body experience and it felt so real. She laid in the bed with my mother's lifeless body and cradled her, rocking her like a baby. She cried from the depths of her soul, begging my mother to wake up, so that she could help her and make everything right. She expressed to my mother how much she needed her and couldn't bear living without her. She ran her fingers through my mother's hair and kissed

her cheeks. Her tears washed away all of my
mother's flaws, and at that moment my mother
was the most beautiful woman I've ever seen.

"As for me, I was frozen. I just looked at
my mother's lifeless body. I was at a loss of
words and emotions. I was so numb and
withdrawn from the world, I didn't know how
to feel. Instead of being able to feel and
properly grieve, my only thoughts were of
giving her a proper burial. Right after she died,
whenever I closed my eyes the image of her
lying there in her bed came back to mind. The
dreams that I have are unbearable. Those
images haunt me even today.

"There was a lot of speculation
surrounding her death. Some say she was
murdered. Some say she committed suicide.
Family members were telling me to get an
autopsy and to demand an investigation. It
was all just too much to bear. I ignored all of

their requests and just let my mother rest in peace.

"How do you feel her death affected you?" asked the therapist. "I see in your journal you wrote that you wished that she was gone so that you would know she was safe."

"That's exactly how I felt and still feel today. My mother wasn't healthy. She did not want to be healthy. It was extremely stressful knowing that my mother was out there in the streets doing, God only knows what. I do feel that now she is in a better place. She isn't hurting herself anymore. She isn't getting beat anymore. She isn't selling her body anymore. My mother lived to kill herself each and every day," I said, holding back tears. "I was affected immensely. How everything took place was a traumatizing experience. On top of having my mother pass away, I had to see her in those conditions. I wasn't told that she was in the apartment. I was under the impression that I was just going to the apartment to do paperwork and from there I would have to go to the morgue to identify her body. That was definitely not the case. One of the biggest factors surrounding her death that affected me most was the fact I didn't get the opportunity to build our relationship. I was never given the chance to love her the way I only dreamed and to feel that she actually loved me in return.

"Her death took a toll on me. I beat myself up, wondering what, if anything, could I have done differently. I wondered if she felt alone. I wondered if she felt any pain. All sorts of thoughts crossed my mind when my mother passed, but they were just that, empty thoughts. Emotionally, I was already withdrawn. Growing up, it seemed as though we never really had a mother, so her death did not affect me the way a mother's death was

supposed to. I didn't cry at her funeral. I had

no more emotions left to give. I had already

been a motherless child for years. Now it was

official.

Chapter Ten

"Sometimes you hit a point where you either change or self-destruct."

~ Sam Stevens ~

I noticed a trend. I kept attracting the same kind of people, people who weren't good for me, who didn't have my best interests at heart, who helped me continue down my destructive path. I especially noticed this with men. I continued to search for what I was missing. My void was still there, more than ever, and I felt that in order to be 100%, it had to be filled. I experienced several relationships that left me in a "wow" state. Was I that preoccupied with attempting to find what I thought was missing that I was blinded by what was right in front of me?

I was dating a guy a few years older than me who owned a house in a Chicago suburb. He told me that he graduated from college and wanted to get into broadcasting. He also worked at a Chicago radio station. What caused us to bond was that we both lost our mothers. When I told him that my mother passed away, he comforted me by sharing his experience about when his mother passed. He was a perfect gentleman towards me.

Come to find out, he wasn't at all who he made himself out to be. He wasn't a few years older, but just the opposite. He didn't own the house where he lived. He never went to college and didn't even work. To put the icing on the cake, his mother was still alive. As a matter of fact, she was the owner of his 'supposed' house. He even lied about his name. Although the relationship was short lived, because the truth showed its beautiful face, I couldn't believe how blind I was. To tell the truth, I knew that something wasn't quite right, but being hopeful, I'd ignored the signs. I was so desperate for love that I turned a blind eye.

Another dysfunctional relationship that I found myself in was with a successful art dealer. This relationship 'had me at hello' because it sparkled and shined. We didn't have regular dates. We would take weekend flights to wherever we wanted to go, just because. Money was never an issue, and that drew me in. The gifts, trips, and unlimited drugs had me in awe. I was on cloud nine, going with the flow of things, but deep down I knew something wasn't right. This guy was nonstop, like he had some type of hyperactive disorder. The drugs and alcohol we consumed, once again, interfered with my better judgment.

This relationship had me so consumed that I was slacking in school. As truth had it, Mr. Art Dealer was a married man. Not only was he married, but he would try and orchestrate different rendezvous with me and other women he met. He was a loose cannon. The thing that grossed me out about this situation wasn't that he was married, because, who was I kidding, I knew men cheated. It was the fact that he was extremely loose with himself on top of being married. Now that I was older and knew better, I had to do better. I dodged many bullets growing up on the street not catching

STD's, and most importantly, AIDS. I wasn't
going to let this man be my demise. It goes to show
you, that everything that glitters isn't gold.

Vegas

I continued going through life in a disarray,
but unbeknownst to me, that would soon come to an
end. My friend and I decided to take a trip to Vegas
for my birthday. We wanted to make sure we had
everything we needed to enjoy ourselves, so we
arranged to have Ecstasy and marijuana waiting for
us when we got there. Everything was going great
and we were having the time of our lives. We
decided to get all dolled up and go to dinner and a
show afterwards. While at the restaurant, we
decided to take the Ecstasy, and after dinner we
went to see the show. While at the show, I started to
feel a little funny. I told my friend and she went to
get me something to drink. By this time, I could no
longer keep seated, so I ran to the bathroom. When I
got into the bathroom, I felt like I was losing my

mind. My body was going through something that I had never before experienced. I needed to scream, cry, laugh, regurgitate and every other act at that very moment just to get some relief from what I was feeling. When the show was over, my friend found me at the back of the theater and could tell that something was wrong with me. We decided to go back to the hotel. When we got into the cab, just like that, my friend started to feel what I was feeling. We were both sick as dogs. We arrived to the hotel and stumbled to our room. My friend threw up everywhere. I still wasn't feeling right. My mind was going a thousand miles per hour, but my body could barely move. I was having a hard time breathing, and I felt like I needed to scratch off my skin just to stop it from crawling. I thought I was going to die that night. I thought that I was going to die from a drug overdose just like my mother. How ironic, I thought. At that point, we were both having a horrible reaction to the drugs that lasted for hours. I prayed to God, asking (begging), if He got me out of this situation that I would never do it again. Not once did I ever do that again.

Chapter Eleven

"If we don't change, we don't grow. If we don't grow, we aren't really living."

~ Gail Sheehy ~

Time for Change

I became tired of the way I was living and I could honestly say that I was ashamed of myself. I was ashamed of how care free I had been with my mind, body, and, most importantly, my soul. I was tired of giving myself away to the highest bidder like I was taught so many years ago. It was time to make a change. My outlook on life started becoming clear. It was as though my eyes were finally opened.

I needed to understand why I thought the way I did. Why was I doing all of these things to myself? Why didn't I care about the things that mattered most? I felt as though I was simply existing and not living. What was my purpose? Why was I here? Did I really go through a lifetime of pain in vain? Although I didn't want to admit it, in fear of looking weak, my upbringing really affected me, and it was time to stop using it as my crutch, and get it together.

Not only did I need to better understand myself, but I also needed to understand what my mother went through. Seeing her lying lifeless in her bed weighed heavily on me. I tried to act as though I had it all together, but truthfully, I was in pain. I never properly healed from my upbringing and the embedded image of my mother in her bed in that condition was devastating. I felt like I was going to explode, like I was losing my mind.

I needed to know how someone could love a drug more than she loved her kids. I knew that once she was addicted she no longer had control, but things like that weren't supposed to happen to me! The little lost girl within screamed 'Mommy why couldn't you be stronger?' Then I looked at myself. I traveled the same destructive path as my mother. Why couldn't I be stronger? Had I turned into my mother?

I needed to understand. I needed to know first-hand why people thought and behaved the way they did. I needed peace, and the only way I was going to get it was by knowing the truth. I needed closure.

"Is this when you decided to go to school for Psychology?" he asked.

"Yes," I replied.

"Right after my mother died I decided to enroll in school for psychology. I needed to learn how and why the brain works as it does."

"How did that work for you?" he asked.

"It worked great. I love Psychology. I loved learning the different theories of how the mind works. I loved being able to get a better understanding of my mother's disease and also learn more about myself. I love not being ignorant to my situation and getting to the root of how one thing affects another."

"That's good. I'm happy to hear that," he replied. "What exactly do you feel you learned about yourself?"

"I learned that the emotions I went through in my life were the same of a person who went through the grieving process. I was grieving for a life I never had, yet longed for."

"That could be possible. Continue."

"You know the five stages of grief: denial, bargaining, anger, depression, and acceptance, right? Well, I can relate to that process. Take for instance, denial. I embraced this stage wholeheartedly. I was in denial for a long time about what I was doing to myself. I tried to convince myself that what I was doing was no big deal and that I was only having fun, but deep down inside I knew better. I've always known better, ever since I was a little girl. I was just trying to numb myself to the realization of what I was doing. I thought if I told myself enough that I wasn't doing anything wrong, then my actions wouldn't bother me as much. Bargaining. I became a pro at bargaining. I used to tell myself all the time that I had the upper hand over my situation(s). I convinced myself that I was using men for what I needed and that I wasn't losing anything in the process. The next stage that I went through, was anger, when I decided enough was enough. During this time in my life I started to examine myself. I examined my actions, my way of thinking, my attitude towards my situation, everything. I became angry and ashamed of myself. This led to my depression. For a while I allowed myself to fall into 'woe is me' mode. I allowed myself to have several pity parties. My anger toward my actions, and that I was weak enough to fall into depression, fueled me to fight back. I forced myself to look at everything I'd been through and make peace with it. I accepted my life and the choices I'd made and I chose to make peace with them, owning them as my own.

"That is a good way to help you understand your process and what you've been through. Actually anything that helps break things down so that you can see them clearly is good."

"It's funny, when I started to write my thoughts and memories, it was therapeutic. I know you mentioned that this was possible, but I didn't think it would be for me. I did not know that by writing how I was feeling and getting it out of my head and onto paper, this would give me a sense of peace. Once on paper I was able to look at each and every thing that I've been through more clearly and in detail, which allowed me to dissect each situation and see why it affected me like it did. I was able to see time and time again how I put myself in danger. I was able to see how I used people to get what I needed, thinking I had the upper hand, when in reality it was them, using me,

allowing them to have the upper hand over
me."

"This is good," he replied. "You are
right. Writing down your thoughts, memories,
fears, and desires can be extremely
therapeutic."

"At first I was embarrassed to share my
life with you, but then I thought, I need to
write everything. I need to help you help me.
After reading everything I've been through
and seeing it in black and white, I knew that it
was time for a change. Having lived my life a
certain way and then consider a completely
different lifestyle was extremely frightening."

"I understand wholeheartedly what you
mean, Christian. Change is hard and is
avoided by most. Being complacent is easy. I
have one last homework assignment for you. I
want you to write more. You already wrote
your experiences. Now I want you to write

about how you feel those experiences affected

you. What did you lose from your experiences?

What did you learn from your experiences? I

want you to express how you think everything

you've been through molded you into the

person you are today; your fears and

insecurities, likes and dislikes. Talk about how

everything affected you. Also, I want you to

write about your children and Paul. I want to

hear a little about them. I want to know how

they have affected you."

"Okay," I replied, with a smile.

Chapter Twelve

"In three words I can sum up
everything I've learned about life:
it goes on."

~ Robert Frost ~

My last homework assignment!

Part 1 - My children

My children. My life. My loves. Raising my children has been one of the most fulfilling experiences life has granted me. I live for my children. I'd rather go through my pain and struggles ten times over before allowing my children to experience it for a day. I want to be able to teach and give my children everything, the world.

My oldest son, Daniel, is my calm child. He is a true gentleman whose intelligence seems effortless. He is smarter than I'll ever be and has the type of personality I wish I had. He is very loving and caring and is extremely handsome. He has the type of smile that brightens up the darkest day. I can honestly say that he is perfect (outside of his messy room). I know that Daniel is going to be someone great in life.

McKenzie, my only girl, is the second oldest. She has the biggest heart of anyone I've ever met in my life. She is one smart cookie and is a true beauty,

inside and out. McKenzie reminds me so much of

myself (her attitude) that it scares me. We already

have so much in common. She's a big reader, like

her mommy, and has already started her own book!

My youngest, Mason, is my little

heartthrob. I couldn't ask for a smarter baby boy.

He is only a year old and has already brightened so

many lives. He already has a little sense of humor

and his presence demands attention wherever he

goes.

My children bring me true joy. They are a

huge part of my motivation to succeed in life. It is

my mission for them to have everything that I

didn't have, and to accomplish this, I am

continuously working on myself so that I can be the

best person possible for them, and provide them

with everything they need: a happy home, the best

education, and love. It is important that my

children have the one thing I regret never having, a

mother. I want them to have a mother they can be proud of, a mother that they can look up to.

Part 2 - Exposed

At a certain point in my life I had two beautiful children, worked full time, and was continuing my studies. I decided to change the way I was living. I needed to regroup and get my thoughts together. I needed to focus on the things that were important to me, my children and school.

There was a time when I thought finding the love of my life would complete me. I later learned that expecting someone else to complete me would create an unhealthy dependency.

I didn't realize it at the time, but I had a resentment towards men. I decided not to engage my thoughts with the possibility of having a relationship because men had consumed my entire life in the past. I didn't think that I would ever be able to have a normal relationship, and I had made peace with this, and believe it or not, it felt refreshing. Yes, at first it was a little heart breaking knowing that I would probably never have a loving relationship and live happily ever after, but it also made me stronger. Knowing that I had to work twice as hard to provide my children with everything I didn't have, made me do the work. It was the best motivation ever.

That's when something extraordinary happened. After I decided that enough was enough and stopped looking for something (anything) to fill my void, I met my Prince in Shining Armor. I guess the saying is true:

When you stop chasing the wrong things you give the right things a chance to catch you. ~ Lolly Daskal ~

One day while on Facebook (Yes, Facebook), I became friends with an interesting fellow. To this day, who requested who is still in question (lol), and will remain forever a mystery. Little did I know how, in the next few months, my life would change. We first made contact when he put up an interesting quote regarding the true riches of life and living life to its fullest, or something to that effect. I sent a message to his inbox to let him know I stole it. Over the next few months we continued to talk here and there. Following several interesting conversations through Facebook, I found myself more than intrigued. One day, in the fall of 2010, the conversation became more interesting. I mentioned on Facebook that I was studying a particular topic in my psychology class and he understood the concept. This caught my attention and I became extremely fascinated by this gentleman. He wasn't like anyone I'd ever met. He helped me with my homework on several occasions and never once asked for anything. It was almost too perfect. I later came to know his heart, and, as we shared a mutual attraction, this love language of service that he shared with me only drew us closer together. He was kind of weird and quirky, but in a good way. Following our previous exchange of offline contact information, several late nights, early morning, and midday conversations ensued. We talked often. It was perfect. His smooth demeanor, charismatic personality, coupled with the tonality of his voice in the evenings and quality conversations kept us talking for hours on end. Many of our conversations were about his travels and his dreams for this world (did I mention I liked people with dreams and aspirations?). I loved this about him. There was something in this that I sought for myself. Like I mentioned before, he was fascinated by what was between my ears: my brain. Something about him was so pure and innocent. I could tell that he wasn't hardened by this world. He was extremely genuine and that drew me in.

This guy wasn't at all what I would consider my type. Looking back at my life's choices of men, I don't think I ever took the time to actually define what it was I wanted in a man. Friends and family members who knew the kind of guys I would typically surround myself with questioned our relationship because they were used to seeing me with men cut from a different cloth, in multiples, and usually for a moment. From age to occupation, I had varied the scales with who I dealt with. In all those years, I had never met anyone who made me feel the way Paul had. I became tired of the way I was living, and, wanting a change, I knew that I had to do something different, and he was it. He was different from anyone I've ever met. Paul made me think, and I loved that feeling.

We first met face to face a few months after the Facebook encounter. After talking to him so long, it seemed as though we'd known each other forever. I didn't know if he was a serial killer, but my gut told me to follow my instincts, so I did. One night, he came over to help me wrap my children's Christmas gifts. This was our first actual "meeting" and we've never parted ways since. This man who was genuine, sincere, innocent, pure, and could have been serial killer, but wasn't, is my Paul.

This relationship wasn't rushed like the rest. We didn't have a relationship based around partying, fornicating, drinking, or doing drugs. We actually dated and got to know each other before we became serious. We sought to learn about each other and we are still learning more about each other every day. I was able to open up to him about my past in detail without fearing judgment. He makes me want to do better and be better.

A year after we met, Paul proposed. Two years after meeting, we had our son, Mason Paul.

I can honestly say that Paul was a breath of fresh air.

Paul and I are in the process of building something great together. We are working towards accomplishing the 'American Dream' to the fullest. That is what life is all about; having a beautiful

family and home, giving, teaching, and loving. To
me it is, and I wanted it all.

Part 3

"The strength of a woman is not
measured by the impact that all her hardships
in life have had on her; but the strength of a
woman is measured by the extent of her refusal
to allow those hardships to dictate her and
who she becomes." ~ C. JoyBell C. ~

What did I lose from my experiences?
In the beginning, I lost my sense of self-
worth. I lost respect for myself. I used my body as a
tool and allowed myself to be used as an object for
men's pleasure. Having to put up a facade my
entire life, I lost my sense of self. I became hardened.
My emotions were put on a back burner. Things
that were supposed to matter and have significance
like love, sex, and relationships, were nothing to me.

My body, mind, and soul were given away without a care in the world. My ability to trust was gone. My ability to see the best in people was nonexistent. I had the frame of mind that you were guilty until proven innocent. I lost my ability to believe and have faith.

I lost a lot from my experiences, but I'm slowly gaining it all back. I'm learning how to appreciate things.

What did I gain?

Growing up fast on the streets was hard, but it left me with the ability to read people. I found this skill was crucial when dealing with random people, because everyone won't have your best interest at heart. There are a lot of wolves in the world dressed in sheep's clothing. I learned to be appreciative. I didn't have a support system growing up. I didn't have people looking out for my well-being. Now, I'm appreciative of everything, and because I know

how hard life can be, I've become extremely giving.
I love helping people.

My insecurities?

My insecurities aren't obvious, but both
mentally and physically, I have my doubts.
Mentally, I'm insecure that I didn't do more with
my life. I know I have so much potential. I wish I'd
done better in school and pushed myself more.
Physically, I was free with my body, yet this
'freedom' left me with a bondage of which I have yet
to entirely escape. I know that I'm human and we
all make mistakes, but I hate that my future
husband knows of my past experiences. Yes, he tells
me that he loves me, flaws and all, but it still
bothers me. I'm insecure about how the mistakes I
made as a teenager haunt me every day. I have old
tattoos everywhere that I try to hide daily. Wearing
tattoos on my body as a daily reminder of my past,

is what I regret the most. It's like a daily kick in the gut.

What are my fears?

I was fearful of becoming like my mother. I was very close at one point. That fear helped me stop going down a destructive path. I'm fearful of my children experiencing even a taste of what I've been through. I'm fearful that I won't be able to change my way of thinking. To be honest, my experiences left me both externally and internally scarred. Because of my past, certain emotions do not come naturally. My mind doesn't work the same as others, and I am fearful that it never will. I am fearful that although most of my scars from my past do not show, they will torture me forever, because they are etched in my soul.

What did I learn?

I've learned a lot in my lifetime. My experiences taught me to value relationships, the value of self-worth, and the value of self-pride. I can say this now, as an adult, after reflecting on the mistakes from which those lessons were learned. I've learned the importance of loving and taking care of my body. Realizing that I only get one, thinking back, had I had the smarts to say no, I would not have damaged my brain so much during my developmental years. I am adamant about improving my mind, and am learning several techniques to drastically improve the quality of the cells left in my brain. Lastly, I've learned that I am only human and that I have to learn to accept my mistakes.

"This is all very good, Christian. Do you realize from writing your experiences you've gotten to the bottom of almost all of your issues?"

"I did realize," I said, with a smile. "At first I was totally against writing my experiences. I thought it was going to be a waste of time, but I see things better now. I just need help fixing me," I said, trying to hold back tears. "I noticed you said 'almost' all of my issues. What does that mean?"

"The thing is, Christian," he said, handing me a tissue. "You're already past the toughest hurdle. You recognized that something was wrong and took action. You're not living life believing that nothing is wrong. You've recognized your flaws and you're seeking help. You're on the right path. Just know, 'deprogramming your way of thinking,' does not happen overnight. It takes time, but you can do it. I have faith in you. There's one last thing that you must do. I know you do not like feeling weak, so you will not admit to certain things. When we first met, you told me that you were not holding on to any anger toward your mother. This may be true, but what I need to know is, have you ever forgiven her?"

"Well, I never thought about it. I guess I have."

"It's not that simple, Christian. The majority of the issues you've expressed are directly related to how you related to your world growing up. Your mother's personal demons, a family divided, and your own personal struggles seems to have affected you in a way you didn't expect. Christian, as difficult as this may be to hear, until you make peace with your past, you will always have that burden on your shoulders. You'll bring these destructive emotions into every situation, relationship, and friendship from here on. For your sake, Christian, I want you to do something."

"Okay." I responded.

"Christian, take this pen and paper and write a quick letter to your mother. The goal of this exercise is to write down those feeling buried deep within and give them a place to reside outside your mind and body. When you're done writing the letter, and please, take as much time as you need, you can either rip up the letter or keep it, the choice is yours. The point is for you to get it out of your mind. You do not need any more weights holding you down. So, if you're willing and ready to write, I'll step out of my office and give you some privacy."

"Yes, I'm ready. Thank you. Thank you so much."

"You're welcome Christian," he said, with that genuine smile.

Dear Mom,

My therapist asked me to write you. The reason why he asked me to write is because we're trying to see if I've ever forgiven you. Truth be told, I don't know. I don't know how I feel. Here I am, a grown ass woman, clueless. Mom, I'm trying, but it's so hard. I'm trying to be healthy for my kids. I'm trying to stay sane, but it's so hard. I'm trying to forget all of the horrible memories that haunt me every day, but it seems impossible. I wish that you could be here for me, Mommy, because I feel so lost, and I am in so much pain. I'm so tired of hurting. I'm so tired of carrying all of this inside. I have to forgive you so that I can finally be FREE.

So here it is, Mommy; I forgive you for everything.

I'm so sorry you had to go through so much. I love you so much and have been carrying around this pain for so long and I can't do it anymore. I have to let it go. Just know that I love you. I've always loved you. Not once did my love waver, then and now.

Mommy, I forgive you, and most importantly, I forgive myself.

Chapter Thirteen

*"If you don't get lost, there's a
chance you may never be found."*

~ Author Unknown~

When I first started writing my memories, it was so my therapist could get a better idea of my story. I needed him to understand where I was coming from so that he could help me. What I didn't expect, was that by helping him, I also helped myself. Going back and looking at everything I've been through, all the men, drugs, and alcohol, being taken advantage of sexually, being self-destructive, all of the physical and mental abuse, has changed my outlook on life. Looking at all I've been able to accomplish since then, makes me hopeful. If I was able to go through it and pull myself out, anyone can.

One cannot control the cards they are dealt in life, but what they can control is how they play them. I know from experience that a person can be their own worst enemy, especially if they fall into the trap of blame or guilt over the hand that life dealt them. When my self-esteem and self-worth were at an all-time low, I thought there was no help for me. I thought that I was going to remain lost forever. I felt like I was stuck in a black hole with no way out, Boy, was I wrong.

The key element that helped pull me out of my destructive lifestyle was becoming closer with God. I've always been a very spiritual person as far as my beliefs, but while making this change, I knew I needed more. For once I had to allow myself to become vulnerable and put everything in God's Hands. With His help, I was able to change my way of thinking. When I changed my way of thinking, I noticed that everything started working in my favor. When I realized my self-worth, the self-respect I lacked my entire life came forth, full force.

I started to see things in myself that I never knew existed. I started to see myself in a new light. I never realized how important my thoughts were. Once I made this miraculous discovery about my patterns of thinking and how they tended to be negative, I knew something had to change. Who and what I associated with on a regular basis had a profound effect on me. I started to eliminate anything in my life that brought up those negative thoughts. The old saying 'If you want to fly, you've got to give up the things that weigh you down,' came to mind. It was hard to accept, but I had faith and allowed God to lead the way.

I learned, whether it be family members, a lover, friends, a stressful job, or anything that had me thinking and feeling negative thoughts, I had to get rid of it. This part may be hard for some, but it is a necessity if you really want to make a change in your life.

Once they're gone, fill the void with positive things. I cut ties with everyone I thought was contributing negatively to my life. I stopped going to the places I knew weren't good for me. I cut off all the men and even some of my friends. I used the time and energy that I would have been wasting with them and threw myself into my studies and my children. I made sure that most of my time was spent on something productive, creating positive thoughts.

My positive thoughts started to take over. I wanted to go further in my education, so for me, there was no other option. I had a point to prove to myself. I was on a mission to free myself from everything I'd come to know. Instead of just an Associate's and a Bachelor's Degree, I received my Master's as well. I told myself that I wanted to be healthier, so I started to take better care of myself. I did not allow myself to stress over everyday worries, but instead focused on the good. I noticed that if I allowed myself to wallow in sorrow for too long, this would cause a domino effect and everything would come crashing down. I was grateful for everything that had made a difference in my current life, and allowed me to have a positive outlook for the future.

Normally, when people tell their story, they tell it from a 'been there, done that' perspective. This isn't that. I'm still healing from my experiences. This is an ongoing journey. I'm not going to say that I have it all together. I'm not going to pretend to be this person, who, after living this tragic life, transformed into this wonderful being. I'm not going to say that my therapist was able to give me the miracle cure that left me golden, because all that would be a lie. Although the therapy sessions were helpful in the start on this journey of getting my thoughts out of my head for further 'analysis,' ultimately, it was the discovery that I was at the root of all that was happening in my present and that it was my relationship with the things that happened in the past that kept me in that past-present place. I discovered that how I was in those moments of my life was not who I am. That discovery alone was one of the most profound. It has led me on a journey of further self-discovery. Even though that moment was life changing, it ultimately won't be all the changes that will take place in my life. I'm not a finished product yet, in fact, this journey is only just beginning. I'm a work in progress. I can't undo the past. But, by focusing my energy and attention on who I ultimately want to be in the future, my actions should follow suit. I decided I would not let my past determine my future nor dictate who and what

I would become. Realizing that my purpose is to help others, I hoped that by sharing my story with the world, I would be a ray of light to at least one person, giving them hope in their situation.

I want people to know they can pull themselves out of any situation, no matter how bad, and to know that with a little faith all things are possible. I hear people complain all the time about how they wasted time and years of their lives because of bad decisions they made. They beat themselves up because they stayed in bad relationships or didn't go to school, etc. What I want to show people, is no matter your situation, your time was not wasted. You took something from every situation, good and bad, and those lessons helped mold the person you are today. We are all human. We all make mistakes. Just remember that falling down is a part of life, and getting back up is living. I feel I was chosen to go through harsh experiences to be an inspiration to others. I feel that I was chosen to be a teacher, in my own right, to show others, with hope and faith, anything is possible. Some of the most beautiful people I've had the pleasure of knowing haven't come from privileged backgrounds, but instead, have experienced suffering, hardships, trials, tribulations, and found their way out, just like me. Thank You, God, for giving me an outlet to share my testimony. Hopefully, it will be that little ray of light to help someone in need.

That is why, Christian Speaks.